ACE YOUR **SHRM** CERTIFICATION EXAM

A Guide to Success on the SHRM-CP® and SHRM-SCP® Exams

D1564529

ACE YOUR SHRM CERTIFICATION EXAM

A Guide to Success on the SHRM-CP® and SHRM-SCP® Exams

Study Guide + Practice Questions

Society for Human Resource Management
Alexandria, Virginia www.shrm.org

Society for Human Resource Management, India
Mumbai, India www.shrmindia.org

Society for Human Resource Management
Haidian District Beijing, China www.shrm.org/cn

Society for Human Resource Management, Middle East and Africa Office
Dubai, United Arab Emirates www.shrm.org/pages/mena.aspx

SHRM®
BETTER WORKPLACES
BETTER WORLD™

This publication is designed to provide accurate and authoritative information regarding the subject matter covered. It is sold with the understanding that neither the publisher nor the author is engaged in rendering legal or other professional service. If legal advice or other expert assistance is required, the services of a competent, licensed professional should be sought. The federal and state laws discussed in this book are subject to frequent revision and interpretation by amendments or judicial revisions that may significantly affect employer or employee rights and obligations. Readers are encouraged to seek legal counsel regarding specific policies and practices in their organizations.

This book is published by the Society for Human Resource Management (SHRM). The interpretations, conclusions, and recommendations in this book are those of the author and do not necessarily represent those of the publisher.

SHRM, the Society for Human Resource Management, creates better workplaces where employers and employees thrive together. As the voice of all things work, workers and the workplace, SHRM is the foremost expert, convener and thought leader on issues impacting today's evolving workplaces. With 300,000+ HR and business executive members in 165 countries, SHRM impacts the lives of more than 115 million workers and families globally. Learn more at SHRM .org and on Twitter @SHRM.

Library of Congress Cataloging-in-Publication Data
Names: Society for Human Resource Management (U.S.), author.
Title: Ace your SHRM certification exam : study guide & practice questions.
Description: First edition. | Alexandria, Virginia : Society for Human Resource Management,
    [2019] | Includes bibliographical references and index.
Identifiers: LCCN 2019019666 (print) | LCCN 2019021635 (ebook) | ISBN 9781586446154
    (pdf) | ISBN 9781586446468 (epub) | ISBN 9781586446178 (mobi) |
    ISBN 9781586446147 (pbk. : alk. paper)
Subjects: LCSH: Personnel management—Examinations—Study guides. | Personnel manage-
    ment—Examinations, questions, etc. | Personnel departments—Employees—Certification.
Classification: LCC HF5549.15 (ebook) | LCC HF5549.15 .A34 2019 (print) | DDC
    658.30076—dc23

Printed in the United States of America   FIRST EDITION

PB Printing   10 9 8 7 6 5 4 3 2 1   SHRMStore SKU: 61.19503

Contents

PART ONE
ABOUT THE SHRM-CP AND SHRM-SCP CERTIFICATION EXAMS

PART TWO
STUDY FOR SUCCESS

PART THREE
SHARPEN YOUR TEST-TAKING SKILLS

List of Graphics

Figures

Tables

Foreword

Congratulations! You're taking a big step toward moving ahead in your career as an HR professional. Choosing to follow an HR career path requires an interest in and dedication to life-long learning. Passing the SHRM certification exam bears witness to your dedication to the field of HR, mastery of HR knowledge and evidence of your ability to use what you know to behave competently in the workplace as an HR leader. Once you earn the SHRM-CP® or SHRM-SCP® credential, recertifying every three years becomes the next critical step toward your continued learning, growth and competence as an HR professional. SHRM hopes you will embrace certification as a critical step in a life-long commitment to knowing, doing, learning and growing as an HR professional. Your commitment to your own growth and development helps you create a better workplace and a better world.

To help you succeed, SHRM has created this study guide. This book will help you understand what SHRM recommends you learn and do to increase your chances of doing well on the exam. Preparing for a test is much like planning a vacation or business trip—the better the plan, the better able you will be to execute that plan, and the more pleasant the entire experience will be.

In this book, we provide tools to guide you on your journey toward success on the SHRM certification exam. We recommend you leverage these resources to succeed. This study guide:

- Provides an easy-to-use guide to help demystify the SHRM Certification exam, with expert tips for understanding, studying, practicing, and reducing pre-test anxiety so you can do your best on the exam.
- Covers everything you need to know about the exam, including development, content, structure, scoring, results, and more.

- Features interviews with experts and tips from real test-takers on preparing for the exam and reducing test anxiety.
- Shows how to create a study plan based on your individual learning style and proven strategies for effective studying.
- Highlights how to best use the practice items included under timed conditions as a realistic preview of the operational exam.
- Includes ready-to-use tools, templates, and worksheets to guide study and practice plans.
- Details learning and study resources, including a guide to the terminology and acronyms commonly used on the exam.

We also include special features that help you focus, organize, and plan your study time before taking the exam. These include:

- Quotes, stories, and advice from former test-takers
- Key point summaries, infographics, and additional information highlighted for quick reference
- Activities, including self-assessments and reflection tools
- Planning tools (e.g., a study-plan template)
- Examples to illustrate core concepts

Our hope is to prepare you to take the exam feeling confident that you have given yourself the best possible chance of passing.

We look forward to becoming and remaining your career partner, and we welcome the opportunity to support you as you learn, grow, know and contribute to your workplace, develop as a professional and advance the HR profession through those contributions. With SHRM certification as the next step on your journey, we wish you success on the exam.

Best of luck in your professional development endeavors, and happy studying!

—Alexander Alonso, PhD, SHRM-SCP
SHRM Chief Knowledge Officer,
Knowledge Development &
Certification, Alexandria, Virginia

Introduction

*The only person you are destined to become
is the person you decide to be.*

—Ralph Waldo Emerson

The SHRM-CP and SHRM-SCP are the first-ever behavioral competency-based certifications for HR generalists, setting a new global standard in certification for the HR profession. By achieving and maintaining SHRM certification, you are making a commitment to lifelong learning about human resources.

Why take the certification exam?

HR professionals who have earned certification say that it enhances their credibility, helps them stay competitive in the job market, increases their confidence, and helps them keep up with developments in the HR field.

Each year, we survey thousands of former test-takers to learn what role certification plays in their career development. Here's what we've found:

- SHRM-certified professionals are more focused on continuous improvement for themselves and their organizations
- SHRM-certified professionals are more employable, are more likely to be promoted, and make more money
- SHRM-certified professionals have a more relevant skill-set, are more productive, and demonstrate more leadership potential

- SHRM-certified professionals feel more satisfied with their careers
- SHRM-certified professionals benefit from ties to a supportive professional community

Why this book?

We've written this book to share what we've learned from successful test-takers about what worked when they prepared for and took the certification exam, including:

- Their insights about what it was like to prepare for a challenging exam
- What they discovered about how their HR experience helped them succeed
- How they created and stuck to a workable study plan and schedule, so they would be ready on test day
- How they managed any feelings of nervousness or anxiety they experienced
- What test-taking strategies they used to help them answer the exam questions

How the book is organized

In Part 1, you'll find an overview of SHRM certification and the SHRM-CP and SHRM-SCP exams; guidance for determining whether you are eligible to take the test and deciding which test to take; and an explanation of how the exams are created, administered and scored.

Part 2 includes an exploration of learning styles, so you can discover how you learn best; proven strategies for studying effectively; and guidance for creating a study plan that makes the most of your study time.

Part 3 covers best practices for successful test-taking that will help you draw on your HR experience and what you learn from studying to answer the questions on the exam.

In Part 4, we address test anxiety, including reasons you might feel anxious or nervous before an important test; the physical symptoms that result from the "flight or fight" response to threats; and strategies for reducing those symptoms.

Part 5 gives you a preview of what to expect when at the testing center, including what happens when you arrive, how to navigate on the testing computer, and how you'll learn your exam result.

How to use this book

There are a variety of ways to prepare for the SHRM certification exams. This study guide is designed to supplement the preparation methods that are the best fit for you.

You can study on your own, using this book as a guide. You can participate in a structured learning program: SHRM offers a comprehensive certification preparation resource, the SHRM Learning System®, in a variety of formats—self-study, virtual or in-person instructor-led programs through SHRM or through partner universities that are authorized to teach the SHRM Learning System content. You can join with other certification candidates to form a study group, many of which form organically through SHRM chapters. Whichever method or methods you choose, a key part of your preparation will be thinking through the types of situations, challenges, problems, and opportunities you encounter in your day-to-day HR work.

A word about graphics and quotes

Throughout the book, you'll find visual examples along with graphics and quotes from former test-takers. The graphics include icons that point you to information that help to set context for a topic, give you interesting facts or provide specific guidance on how to accomplish the various steps needed to apply for the exam, study, get ready for test day, and more. The icons also point you to brief activities that help you think about what you're reading.

Guide to Book Features

 EXPLORE: A pause to reflect where you are and where you'd like to go

 CHECK YOURSELF: Questions to help guide your exam preparation

 QUICK TIPS: Advice from subject matter experts and test-takers

 ONLINE: Additional online resources

 FYI: A deeper dive on topics

A word about how this book was developed

This book is a collaborative effort among the SHRM staff in various divisions, along with expert assistance from a seasoned book writer and editor. There are many moving parts in test development and administration, so each internal expert contributed his or her piece of the puzzle to provide you with a complete picture of the exam, the test-day experience, and what it takes to prepare. Our goal was to provide as much helpful information in one source as possible and to dispel myths about the SHRM certification exams, so you can be ready for success on test day.

A word about what this book is NOT

This book is not a deep dive into the SHRM Body of Competency and Knowledge (BoCK™). But for success on the certification exam, we encourage you to review the BoCK carefully. Here's why:

- The BoCK represents a comprehensive practice analysis—it is detailed and comprehensive because its contents represent the entirety of the practice of HR as validated through research.
- The BoCK is a roadmap to every topic that is considered "fair game" for exam questions. It covers hundreds of topics, and we suggest a focused review to augment and inform your study plan. Keep in mind that there are 160 questions on the exam compared to hundreds if not thousands of concepts presented in the BoCK.
- As you review the BoCK, tag the document in some way to differentiate between the areas you have mastered and those you need to learn more about. Identifying what you do and do not know about the topics covered in the BoCK will help you craft a study plan and strategy that works best for you.
- Finally, this book is not intended to replace rigorous test preparation, but rather to complement SHRM's comprehensive and flexible Learning System for SHRM-CP/SHRM-SCP.

Let's get started!

Acknowledgments

This resource was made possible by the thoughtful and generous advice, guidance and input of many smart and talented subject matter experts, especially:

Lead Editor

Nancy A. Woolever, MAIS, SHRM-SCP, Vice President, Certification Operations

SHRM Test Development

Scott Oppler, PhD, Vice President, Exam Development and Research
Alexander Alonso, PhD, SHRM-SCP, Chief Knowledge Officer

SHRM Learning System

Susie Davis, Director, Digital Education
Eddice L. Douglas, SHRM-CP, Specialist, Certification Educational Products
Jeanne Morris, Director, Education Programs
Nick Schacht, SHRM-SCP, Chief Global Development Officer

SHRM Certification Community

Patricia Byrd, Director, Certification Relations

James Connors, Senior Specialist, Certification Communications

Development & Research

Janis Fisher Chan, Lead Writer and Developmental Editor

We also gratefully acknowledge the scores of SHRM members, test-takers, and exam candidates who volunteered to share their stories and offer tips for *Ace Your SHRM Certification Exam*!

Part One

About the SHRM-CP and SHRM-SCP Certification Exams

Without continual growth and progress, such words as improvement, achievement, and success have no meaning.

—Benjamin Franklin

CHECK YOURSELF

Why are you taking this exam?
(Mark all that apply)

❑ Required by my company

❑ Become better at my job

❑ Advance my career

❑ Make myself more employable

❑ Improve my credibility and professional standing

❑ Become part of a professional community

❑ Other:

Chapter 1
The Exam and What It Tests

Live as if you were to die tomorrow.
Learn as if you were to live forever.

—Mahatma Gandhi

The SHRM certification exam tests your capabilities in both aspects of HR practice—competencies and knowledge—that are required for effective job performance. The exam is based upon the core set of competencies and knowledge outlined in the SHRM Body of Competency and Knowledge™ (SHRM BoCK).

A product of rigorous research involving thousands of HR professionals, the BoCK identifies eight key behavioral competencies and 15 HR functional areas that are critical to the success of any HR professional. The BoCK will be your study outline as you prepare for the exam.

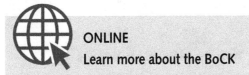

ONLINE
Learn more about the BoCK

Download the SHRM Body of Competency and Knowledge (BoCK): https://www.shrm.org /certification/about/BodyofCompetencyKnowledge /Pages/Download-SHRM-BoCK.aspx

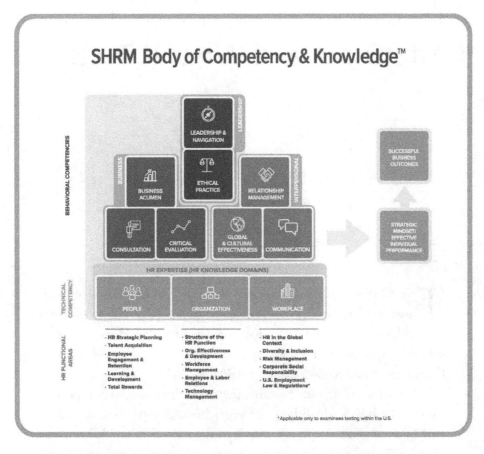

Figure 1.1. Know Your BoCK!

Two certification exams

SHRM offers two levels of certification: the SHRM-CP and the SHRM-SCP. Which exam you take depends on which certification aligns most closely with your job responsibilities and level of experience, and whether you meet the specific eligibility requirements.

- The SHRM-CP is designed for HR professionals who are engaged primarily in operational roles—implementing policies, serving as the HR point-of-contact for staff and stakeholders, and/or performing day-to-day HR functions. HR professionals with one to five years of experience should take this exam.

- The SHRM-SCP is designed for senior HR professionals who operate primarily in strategic roles—developing policies and strategies, overseeing the execution of HR operations, analyzing performance metrics, and/or contributing to the alignment of HR strategies to organizational goals. HR professionals with six or more years of experience should take this exam.

Are you eligible?

SHRM certification is designed for HR professionals who have achieved a certain level of knowledge, skills, and abilities as specified in the exam's eligibility requirements. The critical factor in determining eligibility is your HR-related work experience in the 15 functional areas of HR knowledge in combination with your highest level of education completed. Before applying to take the certification exam, make sure that you have the combination of education and HR-related work experience to be eligible.

QUICK TIP
Student Eligibility

Some students in the final year of an undergraduate or graduate degree program might be eligible to take the certification exam. Your college or university must be aligned to SHRM's curriculum guidelines, and you need at least 500 hours of HR experience through an internship or other work opportunities. You cannot apply directly; your application must be submitted through your institution. Learn more at https://www.shrm.org/certification/apply/EligibilityCriteria/Pages/student-shrm-cp-eligibility.aspx

Table 1.1. SHRM-CP and SHRM-SCP Eligibility

Credential	Less than a Bachelor's Degree*		Bachelor's Degree		Graduate Degree	
	HR-Related Program	Non-HR Program	HR-Related Degree	Non-HR Degree	HR-Related Degree	Non-HR Degree
SHRM-CP*	3 years in HR role	4 years in HR role	1 year in HR role	2 years in HR role	Currently in HR role	1 year in HR role
SHRM-SCP	6 years in HR role	7 years in HR role	4 years in HR role	5 years in HR role	3 years in HR role	4 years in HR role

* Less than a bachelor's degree includes: working toward a bachelor's degree, associate's degree, some college, qualifying HR certificate program, high school diploma, or GED. Eligibility windows are regularly updated at https://www.shrm.org/certification/apply /Pages/default.aspx.

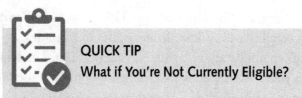

QUICK TIP
What if You're Not Currently Eligible?

If you do not currently meet the eligibility requirements for the certification exam you wish to take, consider what you need to become eligible and create a plan to meet the requirements. You are likely to need more HR-related work experience; if so, becoming eligible is just a matter of time. If you include achieving SHRM certification in your overall development plan and map out a strategy to achieve it, becoming eligible will be within reach.

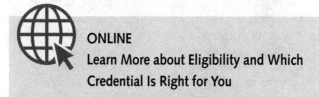

ONLINE
Learn More about Eligibility and Which Credential Is Right for You

https://www.shrm.org/certification/apply /EligibilityCriteria/Pages/default.aspx

How to apply

As of this writing, SHRM offers both certification exams during two testing windows every year at 450 testing centers, with 5,500 seats daily in more than 160 countries. The first window is from May 1 to July 15 and the second is from December 1 to February 15. Once you have decided which exam to take, you can register on the SHRM web site anytime between the Applications Accepted starting date and the Regular Application Deadline. Late registrations are accepted through the Late Application Deadline for an additional fee.

To register, you will:

1. Create a user account
2. Select which exam to take
3. Complete the application form and sign the SHRM Certification Candidate Agreement
4. Pay the registration fee
5. Once you receive your Authorization-to-Test (ATT) letter, schedule your exam using the various approaches outlined in the letter

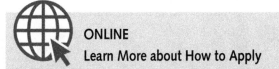

ONLINE
Learn More about How to Apply

https://www.shrm.org/certification/apply/Pages
/applicationprocess.aspx

Table 1.2. SHRM Certification Exam Windows

2019 Winter Exam Window: Dec. 1, 2019–Feb. 15, 2020		
APPLICATIONS ACCEPTED	REGULAR APPLICATION DEADLINE	LATE APPLICATION DEADLINE
May 13	Oct. 18	Nov. 9

The testing windows are the dates during which the exams are administered. The regular application deadline dates are the dates during which candidates can register for the exam. Candidates who apply during the late application period will incur a nonrefundable late fee. Please note exam application deadlines end at 11:59 PM, Eastern Time.

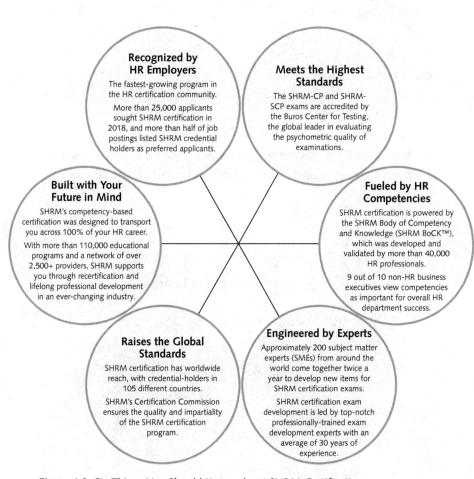

Recognized by HR Employers

The fastest-growing program in the HR certification community.

More than 25,000 applicants sought SHRM certification in 2018, and more than half of job postings listed SHRM credential holders as preferred applicants.

Meets the Highest Standards

The SHRM-CP and SHRM-SCP exams are accredited by the Buros Center for Testing, the global leader in evaluating the psychometric quality of examinations.

Built with Your Future in Mind

SHRM's competency-based certification was designed to transport you across 100% of your HR career.

With more than 110,000 educational programs and a network of over 2,500+ providers, SHRM supports you through recertification and lifelong professional development in an ever-changing industry.

Fueled by HR Competencies

SHRM certification is powered by the SHRM Body of Competency and Knowledge (SHRM BoCK™), which was developed and validated by more than 40,000 HR professionals.

9 out of 10 non-HR business executives view competencies as important for overall HR department success.

Raises the Global Standards

SHRM certification has worldwide reach, with credential-holders in 105 different countries.

SHRM's Certification Commission ensures the quality and impartiality of the SHRM certification program.

Engineered by Experts

Approximately 200 subject matter experts (SMEs) from around the world come together twice a year to develop new items for SHRM certification exams.

SHRM certification exam development is led by top-notch professionally-trained exam development experts with an average of 30 years of experience.

Figure 1.2. Six Things You Should Know about SHRM Certification

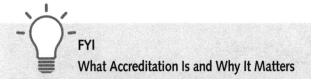

FYI
What Accreditation Is and Why It Matters

Accreditation for a credentialing program provides important corroboration of the program's quality and rigor as determined by an independent, qualified third party. The SHRM-CP and SHRM-SCP are accredited by the Buros Center for Testing at the University of Nebraska, Lincoln.

The Buros Center evaluates the psychometric quality of credentialing testing programs like ours. The center conducts a general audit of the program's processes and procedures along with a yearly, focused evaluation of specific testing windows within the program. SHRM participates in both types of accreditation audit—the periodic general audit and the annual focused testing-year evaluation.

Buros reviews SHRM's policies and procedures to ensure the SHRM-CP and SHRM-SCP maintain a standard of quality as measured by the testing industry. Its review is based on the extent to which SHRM's testing program demonstrates that it meets the Buros Standards for Accreditation of Testing Programs. At the end of each audit phase, Buros provides evidence that the SHRM-CP and SHRM-SCP exams adhere to those standards, along with ways in which the policies or procedures could be modified or improved to meet the expectations of the professional community.

The Buros Standards are periodically updated to reflect current guidelines from the testing community. In particular, the Center's Standards are highly consistent with the 2014 Standards for Educational and Psychological Testing, jointly published by the American Educational Research Association (AERA), the American Psychological Association (APA), and the National Council on Measurement in Education (NCME). The Buros National Advisory Council unanimously approved the revised standards in June 2017. SHRM provides information annually to maintain its accreditation for the SHRM-CP and SHRM-SCP certifications.

—Nancy Woolever, SHRM-SCP

EXPLORE

Which SHRM certification is right for you, the SHRM-CP or SHRM-SCP?

_____

_____

Are you currently eligible to take the exam? If not, what will you do to become eligible?

_____

_____

_____

_____

_____

_____

Chapter 2

Exam Structure and Administration

In failing to prepare, you are preparing to fail.

—Benjamin Franklin

An important part of preparing yourself for the test is knowing what kinds of questions you'll be asked and how the test will be administered. That's what we cover in this section.

No trick questions!

First and foremost, there are no "trick" questions on the SHRM certification exams. You receive credit for each correct answer, and you are not penalized for choosing the wrong answers so there is no penalty for guessing.

Contrary to what is discussed frequently on social media, it's also very important to understand there are no "SHRM" answers. Test questions are written by, edited by, reviewed by, and the answers selected by SHRM-certified HR professionals. The SHRM staff provides expertise in test development, not HR subject-matter expertise. Thus, SHRM relies on thousands of SHRM-certified subject matter experts to create the actual test content. This is why there is no "SHRM" answer. Put that thought aside immediately and permanently; the SHRM answer does not exist!

Three types of test items

The certification exam consists of 160 questions. There are three types of test items:

- Knowledge items (KIs), which test your knowledge of key concepts and terms in the HR field
- Situational judgment items (SJIs), which test your ability to choose the best course of action in relation to the real-life HR situations presented in the question
- Field-test items, including both KIs and SJIs, which are used to test items being considered for future exams

Knowledge-based items

You'll be asked to answer two categories of knowledge-based items (KIs), HR-specific knowledge items and foundational knowledge items.

HR-specific knowledge items cover key concept topics associated with the 15 HR functional areas defined in the BoCK. Foundational knowledge items cover the key topics considered foundational to the eight behavioral competencies.

Each knowledge-based item has only one irrefutably right answer. You receive credit for correct answers; you are not penalized for incorrect responses or for guessing.

Situational judgment items

Situational judgment items are different. For situational judgment items (SJIs), you will be asked to read a realistic, work-related scenario and select the best of several possible strategies to resolve or address the issues. The scenarios are written by SHRM-certified HR professionals based on their actual workplace experiences.

Unlike knowledge-based items, situational judgment items have no one "right" answer, only degrees of effectiveness, based on the judgment of a group of subject matter experts. While more than one of the possible strategies might be effective, one will be best, given the situation and as decided by a panel of SHRM-certified HR professionals. You receive credit only for choosing the most effective course of action;

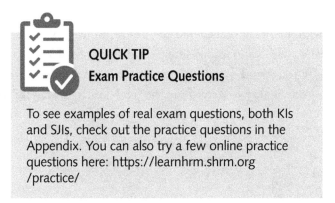

QUICK TIP
Exam Practice Questions

To see examples of real exam questions, both KIs and SJIs, check out the practice questions in the Appendix. You can also try a few online practice questions here: https://learnhrm.shrm.org /practice/

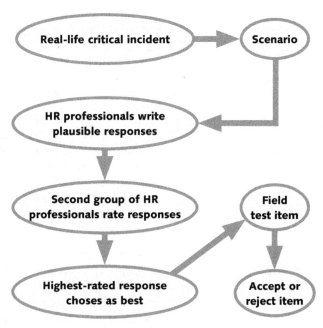

Figure 2.1. How Situational Judgment Items (SJIs) Are Created

again, you will not be penalized for selecting an ineffective response or for guessing.

Field-test questions

There are 30 field-test questions on the exam. Field-test items are randomly mixed with other items and are not counted toward your score.

SHRM uses the field-test items to assess the effectiveness and quality of questions being considered for future exams. Taken as a group, responses to field-test questions help to identify possible content additions to the exam and support growth of the certification program by assessing item quality to determine the field-test item's eligibility to be retained in the item bank and to be placed on a future test form.

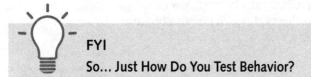

FYI

So... Just How Do You Test Behavior?

SHRM's certification exams use situational judgment items to assess abilities that are defined in the behavioral competencies included in the BoCK. For the HR profession, behaving competently is inextricably linked to HR knowledge. Thus, situational judgment items allow certification candidates to use what they know to demonstrate how to behave competently in a given situation.

For SHRM-CP and SHRM-SCP test-takers, an effective way to think about situational judgment items is to reflect on what occurs in the workplace day-in and day-out. That means thinking about how your behavior affects the outcome of any given situation at work—whether it is solving an employee relations issue, leading a strategic initiative to work out the details of a future-focused workforce development plan or creating a business continuity plan to safeguard the organization from risk.

These types of situations require you as an HR professional to combine knowledge and behavior in the eight behavioral competencies outlined in the BoCK to lead ethically and to communicate, consult, and manage relationships effectively. For that reason, the situational judgment items on the exam ask you to select the most effect course of action presented in the four possible response options.

—Nancy Woolever, SHRM-SCP

How the exam is administered

The SHRM-CP and SHRM-SCP exams are administered via computer at highly secure Prometric testing centers worldwide. Once your application has been accepted, you will schedule your exam on the Prometric web site or by calling Prometric directly.

The total testing time is 4 hours and 15 minutes, which includes 15 minutes for opening and closing activities and 4 hours for the exam itself. There will be a countdown timer on the computer screen, so you can keep track of how much time you have left.

See Part 5 for in-depth discussion of the exam experience.

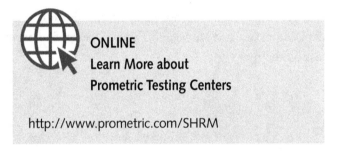

ONLINE
Learn More about
Prometric Testing Centers

http://www.prometric.com/SHRM

How the exam is scored

SHRM uses a rigorous scoring process for certification exams, which includes third-party independent validation and verification. Passing scores are set using the Modified Angoff method, a best-practice procedure commonly used for setting performance standards for certification and licensing exams.

Your performance will be measured against a pre-determined standard, not against that of other people taking the test. To maintain the integrity of the Certification Program, the SHRM Certification Commission evaluates the scoring standard recommendations and ensures the technical quality of all test scoring practices.

After you have finished the test, the system calculates a provisional pass/did not pass result, posts a statement on your screen, and emails the provisional pass/did not pass result to the email address you used when scheduling your testing appointment. You will receive the official results about 4 weeks after you take the test.

If you have a passing score, you will receive an official congratulatory letter, your credential certificate, and a lapel pin. You will also receive a Candidate Feedback Report, which shows your official score, along with information about your performance on the three behavioral competency clusters and three HR knowledge domains. That information can help you select which professional development activities to pursue in order to advance your career and maintain your certification.

If you don't pass

Don't feel discouraged if you do not pass the certification exam. It is a very challenging exam, and between 30 and 45 percent of exam-takers do not pass on the first try.

Figure 2.2. Sample Candidate Score and Feedback Report (Part 1)

Leverage the information on your candidate feedback report—view the experience as a learning opportunity and use your feedback to refocus or re-engineer a study plan that will help you prepare for re-taking the test. You can re-take the exam as often as you wish by completing a new application, meeting all the eligibility requirements, and paying the exam fee.

Maintain your certification

Achieving certification sets you on the path to continuous learning and career development. Maintaining certification helps you keep your knowledge, skills, and abilities relevant.

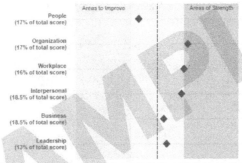

Scores within the grey zone represent test content for which your level of performance was close to that expected of a minimally competent certified HR professional, while scores within the blue zone represent areas of strength (i.e., test content for which your performance was well above that level). In comparison, scores within the yellow zone represent test content for which your performance indicates the greatest need for improvement. Note that distance from the dotted line provides an approximate measure of how far above or below the competence standard for that area your performance on the exam fell. Percentages in parentheses represent the score weighting for each subject area (i.e., how much of your total test score came from each domain).

Areas to Improve | Areas of Strength

People
(17% of total score)

Organization
(17% of total score)

Workplace
(16% of total score)

Interpersonal
(18.5% of total score)

Business
(18.5% of total score)

Leadership
(13% of total score)

SHRM treats our certification score and developmental feedback as confidential, and provides these to you for your own developmental purposes only. Examination scores and feedback will not be disclosed by SHRM to anyone without candidate consent, unless required by law enforcement or judicial authorities. If you would like your examination results to be released to a third party person or organization, you must provide SHRM with a written request that specifically identifies the type of information (e.g., examination date, score, pass/fail status, etc.) about the examination results that the third-party should receive.

Thank you for your dedication to the HR profession and for becoming one of more than 106,000 HR professionals who have chosen to accelerate their careers by earning the SHRM-CP or SHRM-SCP credential. If you have questions, please contact the SHRM Certification team via e-mail at shrmcertification@shrm.org or via telephone at +1.703.548.3440, or +1.703.548.3440 outside the U.S.

Sincerely,

Alexander Alonso, Ph.D., SHRM-SCP
Chief Knowledge Officer
Society for Human Resource Management

Figure 2.2. Sample Candidate Score and Feedback Report (Part 2)

To maintain your certification, you will need to earn 60 Professional Development Credits within each three-year period. Credits are awarded for your study, your experience, and your contributions in three categories: Education, Profession and Your Organization. You can also earn recertification by re-taking the certification exam.

QUICK TIP
Stay Certified!

Plan now to recertify so you do NOT have to take the Certification exam again! There are more than 110,000 opportunities with 2,500+ providers to earn Professional Development Credits (PDCs)—including attending events, volunteering, completing major work projects and reading books!

Visit the SHRM recertification page online to learn more now about the types of activities that earn you PDCs. Don't overlook the importance of volunteering—serving in a volunteer leadership role for a SHRM chapter or state council or even as a volunteer involved in supporting SHRM test development is an important way to supplement professional development education.

Though all 60 credits can be earned by attending virtual or in-person professional development programs, many certified professionals also choose to document a major work project completed and endorsed by their supervisor to earn up to 20 PDCs.

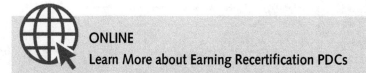

ONLINE
Learn More about Earning Recertification PDCs

Read all about the various categories, what kind of documentation to submit, and how many PDCs can be earned, by category:
https://www.shrm.org/certification/recertification
/RecertificationRequirements/Pages/default.aspx

Part Two

Study For Success

By admitting your inadequacies, you show that you're self-aware enough to know your areas for improvement —and secure enough to be open about them.

—Adam Grant

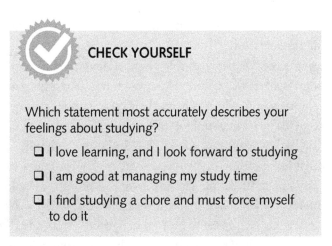

CHECK YOURSELF

Which statement most accurately describes your feelings about studying?

❑ I love learning, and I look forward to studying

❑ I am good at managing my study time

❑ I find studying a chore and must force myself to do it

To succeed on the SHRM-CP or SHRM-SCP exam, you have to know the subject matter that is being tested: the competencies and knowledge outlined in the BoCK. There are two key ingredients. The first is your experience in the HR field. The second is a carefully designed and implemented study plan.

Start with your HR experience. Think about your job: what you do day in and day out, the different kinds of situations you deal with, the fires you put out, the problems you solve, the initiatives you help to create. Consider the HR areas you are already familiar with because of your work: risk management, recruitment, workforce development, compensation plans, and more—all topics that are covered in the BoCK.

> I studied for the SHRM-SCP for one year on my own and attended a free study group at a local college as the exam got closer.

Then create a study plan that will help you close the gaps between what you already know about HR and what you need to know to become a SHRM-certified HR professional. The better you have mastered the HR competencies and knowledge through experience and study, the better prepared you will be to pass the exam.

Start early!

Wouldn't it be nice to have unlimited time to prepare for the certification exam? "Sure," you think, "but I'm already so busy. How am I going to find the time to study?"

Creating time for study in a busy schedule is one reason why it's important get started well ahead of your exam date. According to SHRM statistics, most people who study on their own without taking a course spend 41–80 hours studying for the certification exam. Those who achieve the highest pass rate spend 81–120 hours studying. The average certification candidate spends a total of 70–80 hours preparing for the test, and most people start at least 3–4 months ahead of time. Approximately 10%–15% of that time is spent identifying weak areas.

But everyone is different. How much time you'll need depends partly on how much you already know through your education and experience and partly on how you prefer to learn. The strategies in this section can help you make the best use of your study time, so you will be well-prepared and full of confidence on test day.

Chapter 3

Learning How You Learn Best

Knowing yourself is the beginning of all wisdom.

—Aristotle

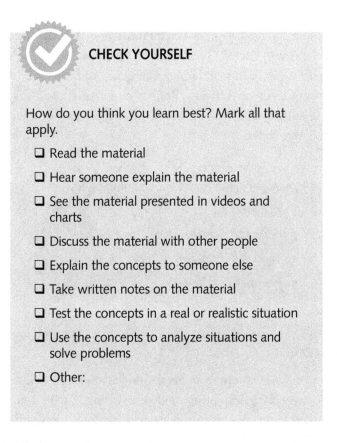

CHECK YOURSELF

How do you think you learn best? Mark all that apply.

- ❏ Read the material
- ❏ Hear someone explain the material
- ❏ See the material presented in videos and charts
- ❏ Discuss the material with other people
- ❏ Explain the concepts to someone else
- ❏ Take written notes on the material
- ❏ Test the concepts in a real or realistic situation
- ❏ Use the concepts to analyze situations and solve problems
- ❏ Other:

W e're not all the same when it comes to learning (and in so many other ways as well!). We receive and process information differently, and we like to learn in different ways.

Some people learn best by reading, taking notes by hand, and explaining the concepts to someone else. Others grasp new information and concepts more easily when the content is presented in visual form, via charts, graphs, slides or videos.

Understanding your learning preferences, or styles, will help you decide how best to study for success on the exam.

Four primary learning styles

In 1982, management experts Peter Honey and Alan Mumford published a Learning Styles Questionnaire based on psychologist David Kolb's learning style model. Honey and Mumford identified four primary types of learners: Activists, Reflectors, Theorists, and Pragmatists. No one is entirely one type or another, but most people prefer one or two of the four styles.

Honey and Mumford: Four Learning Styles
- Activists (Doers)
- Reflectors (Reviewers or Observers)
- Theorists (Thinkers)
- Pragmatists (Planners)

Activists (Doers)

If you're an activist, you have an open-minded approach to learning and enjoy experimenting, exploring, and discovering. Anxious to practice what you learn and apply it to real-world situations, you might become impatient with lengthy discussions and explanations. Some activists might have a tendency to be disorganized and to procrastinate.

Reflectors (Reviewers or Observers)

Reflectors prefer to learn by watching or listening. If you're a reflector, you like to take your time, collect data, and examine experiences or concepts from a number of different perspectives before coming to conclusions. You might have a tendency to dislike pressure and tight deadlines.

Theorists (Thinkers)

If facts, models, concepts and systems help you engage in the learning process, you might be described as a theorist. You like to think things through, analyze what you are learning, and understand the underlying theory. You might also tend to be more organized than other types of learners.

Pragmatists (Planners)

You might describe yourself as a pragmatist if you enjoy solving problems and sometimes become impatient with too much theory and lengthy discussions. When you learn, you want to know how the concepts apply in the "real" world.

Write out the info by hand (this helped me impress it on the brain better than typing it into a computer).

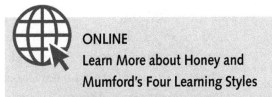

ONLINE
Learn More about Honey and
Mumford's Four Learning Styles

https://www2.le.ac.uk/departments
/doctoralcollege/training/eresources/teaching
/theories/honey-mumford

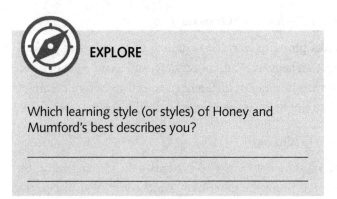

EXPLORE

Which learning style (or styles) of Honey and Mumford's best describes you?

_____

_____

Three ways to learn

Researchers have also found that our learning styles differ in the ways in which we use our senses to receive and process information. One well-known theory, called "VAK," postulates that most of us learn best when using one or two of our three primary sensory receivers: visual, auditory, or kinesthetic.

> I studied. And studied. And studied every chance and moment I got. I am not the best reader, so it was difficult for me to read through the material and grasp it. I don't learn that way. I studied every day whenever I could for a solid three months.

Visual learners

If you're a visual learner, you like to have information presented through pictures, charts, diagrams, lists of key learning points, infographics, videos and other visual media. Taking notes and making visual maps helps you remember what you hear or read. Interestingly, some visual learners can visualize pages on which certain information appears.

Auditory learners

You know that you are primarily an auditory learner if you remember more of what you learn when you hear something than when you see it. You might prefer lectures and podcasts to reading. Reading aloud to yourself or talking about what you learn to other can help fix facts and concepts in your mind.

Kinesthetic learners

You can be described as a kinesthetic learner if you find it hard to sit still for long periods. You need to stand up and move around often to keep from losing your concentration. Keeping study period short and focused, taking notes by hand, and building frequent breaks into your study schedule can help you learn.

The VAK: Three Ways to Learn

- Visual
- Auditory
- Kinesthetic

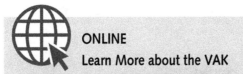

ONLINE
Learn More about the VAK

Sometimes called "VARK" model at https://www .ccconline.org/vakvark-model/

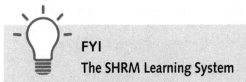

FYI

The SHRM Learning System

The SHRM Learning System offers a variety of formats and tools to help you prepare for the SHRM-CP or SHRM-SCP certification exam. Approximately two-thirds of certification candidates use the Learning System, and those candidates consistently beat the average pass rate.

SHRM has designed several learning options to suit different learning styles, schedules, group sizes and locations. In addition to live and virtual instructor-led options, the Learning System is available through Self-Study. Real-life situations that require decision-making skills are incorporated into the online learning modules in addition to study tools to help you better understand, apply and engage with behavioral competencies and HR knowledge.

Table 3.1 below shows all the formats, so you can choose those that best fit your learning styles and preferences.

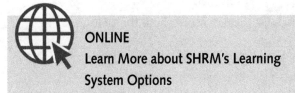

ONLINE

Learn More about SHRM's Learning System Options

https://www.shrm.org/certification/prepare/Pages/default.aspx

Table 3.1. SHRM Learning System Formats

APPROVED SHRM EDUCATION PARTNERS	SHRM EDUCATIONAL PROGRAMS	SELF-STUDY PROGRAM	ONSITE TRAINING & DEVELOPMENT
A traditional classroom setting, online format or a hybrid of the two—over a period of weeks or in a condensed format, led by a local, trusted training provider.	A virtual or in-person classroom environment with interactive and comprehensive discussions, activities and preparation techniques from a SHRM-certified, expert instructor.	Study with our learning tools, where and how you want. Use study tools to customize your learning.	Customized staff training at your location, virtually, or a hybrid of the two—eliminating costly travel expenses and time away from the office.
Ideal for *those who prefer a structured learning environment.*	**Ideal for** *those who prefer a structured learning environment.*	**Ideal for** *those who prefer to learn on their own schedule.*	**Ideal for** *organizations who are looking for a flexible education option.*

EXPLORE

Which of your primary sensory receivers, visual, auditory, or kinesthetic, best helps you learn? Mark them in order.

_____ Visual

_____ Auditory

_____ Kinesthetic

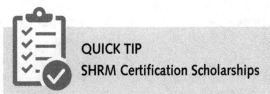

QUICK TIP

SHRM Certification Scholarships

Sponsor: Certification scholarships are offered by the SHRM Foundation (https://www.shrm.org /foundation/ourwork/scholarships/certification /pages/default.aspx)

Scholarship: $750 for SHRM Certification exam and preparation (SHRM-CP or SHRM-SCP)

Number: Minimum of 220 scholarships distributed per year

Application Opens: January 15 or June 1

Deadline: April 15 or September 1

Results Notification: June 15 or November 1

Terms of Use: Expires within 12 months of issue date

- June 15 awards must be used between June 15, 2019 and June 15, 2020

- November 1 awards must be used between November 1, 2019 and November 1, 2020

Chapter 4

Use Proven Study Strategies

Success is not final, failure is not fatal:
it is the courage to continue that counts.

—Winston Churchill

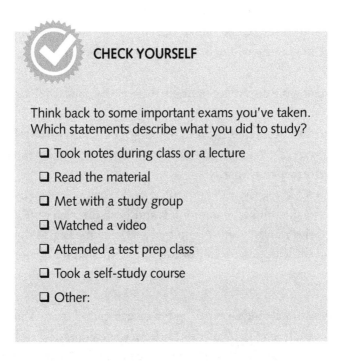

CHECK YOURSELF

Think back to some important exams you've taken.
Which statements describe what you did to study?

❏ Took notes during class or a lecture

❏ Read the material

❏ Met with a study group

❏ Watched a video

❏ Attended a test prep class

❏ Took a self-study course

❏ Other:

It's probably been a while since you've had to study for an important exam. To prepare for the certification exam, you need to get back into "study mode." The strategies in this chapter can make the difference between just studying and studying in a way that will pay off on exam day.

Keep a positive mindset

Imagine that two actors are preparing for the role of a lifetime. The actors are similar in terms of experience and skills. Which of them has the best chance of ending up with an award-winning performance?

Actor #1. He worries that he isn't ready. Maybe, he thinks, he was cast in the role by mistake. Maybe he's just not good enough, and in time, everyone will notice and wish they had cast someone else.

Actor #2. She firmly believes that this role is perfect for her. It will be a lot of work, she thinks, but she can't wait to get started, and she knows she will deliver a stunning performance.

There is a big difference between these two actors. It's their attitude.

Actor #1 approaches the role thinking, "I can't do this." With that attitude, chances are that he won't deliver more than a mediocre performance, if that.

Actor #2 has a very different mindset. Trusting her experience and skills, she thinks, "I *can* do this, and I can do it very well!" Her positive mindset sets her up for success as she begins the long and difficult process of learning the script and rehearsing for the role.

In terms of attitude, preparing for a certification exam is not unlike learning an acting role: If you don't believe you can pass, you set yourself up for failure. Negative thoughts like, "I can't do this" and "other people are much better than I am" make it hard to study and to remember what you've learned on exam day.

But if you approach test preparation with trust in your experience and skills and the belief that you *can* do well, chances are that you will.

You'll find it easier to put in the work to learn the material, cope with the frustrations that learning often involves, and step out of the wings on exam day prepared to deliver the performance of your life!

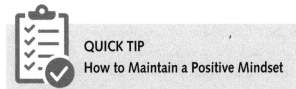

QUICK TIP
How to Maintain a Positive Mindset

- Trust your experience and skills
- Think "I can" instead of "I can't"
- Avoid comparing yourself to others
- See the learning process as an opportunity, not a chore
- Commit yourself to the study process and make it a top priority

Learn actively, not passively

Let's go back to the example of the actors. Actor #2 is approaching the preparation process with a positive mindset. But what if all she does to prepare is read the script and try to memorize the lines silently to herself? It's a good bet that she won't do a very good job. In fact, she's likely to forget many of the lines when she steps on the stage.

That's why actors prepare by reading their lines aloud, thinking about how their characters react to different situations, and rehearsing the scenes over and over again. In other words, the actors learn *actively*, not passively.

Learning experts know that passive learning, such as reading and re-reading, highlighting, rote memorization, listening to lectures and watching videos isn't enough for learners to be able to retain it. Like the actors, being able to retain the material and then to recall it when you need it requires active learning. That means *doing something* with the material.

To learn actively:

- Read to remember
- Look up unclear words and phrases
- Develop outlines of the key facts and concepts
- Use flash cards to help learn key terminology and facts
- Explain and teach the material to others
- Discuss the material with other learners

FYI
Active Recall

The process of learning in a way that helps you remember the information is sometimes called "Active Recall." It's based on the principle that in order to learn and remember the material, you need to stimulate your brain to recall it from your long-term memory when you need it—for example, when you're taking an exam.

Read to remember

Reading is an essential part of studying. But unless you have a photographic memory, you probably forget all or most of what you read by the time you get back from a coffee break.

To study effectively, you have to be able to remember what you read. There are a variety of ways to do that.

Skim what you're about to read

Before you dive into reading a chapter or a section of the material, skim it. Don't try to understand or retain anything at that point—the purpose is to get an overview or a preview of the contents. Notice headings, text that is in boldface or italic type, and bulleted and numbered lists. Anything that is highlighted or stands out gives you clues to the content.

Take smart notes

Notetaking is a time-honored study tool. Taking notes helps you stay focused and engaged in the material, think critically about what you read, draw conclusions, and identify main ideas. But smart note-taking is more than dutifully copying from the text. The way you take notes should help you learn.

Here are some smart note-taking strategies to try:

- **Read a short section**—a couple of paragraphs, up to a page. Without looking back at the text, make notes from what you remember, trying to capture the main points in your own words. Then read the section again and fill in any important details you may have missed.
- **Annotate the text.** If you're reading something in print or using an electronic version that allows commenting, underline, circle, or highlight key words and phrases, and add your own comments.
- **Look up unfamiliar words.** It's very important to understand the terminology that you will find on the test. As you read, look up any words or acronyms you don't fully understand. Note the definition on the page and keep a separate list of terminology you need to study. Use the acronym list and glossary in the appendix of this book and in the BoCK to review the meaning of key terms and concepts.
- **Stop from time to time and think about what you're reading.** Is the concept new to you, or are you already familiar with it from your own experience? In what ways might it be used or applied in the real world or on the exam? Remember that the situational judgment items on the exam are based on critical incidents encountered by HR professionals—the kinds of incidents you regularly have to handle at work. Consider how the concepts relate to situations you've already experienced in your job.
- **Write summaries.** Writing a summary in your own words helps you focus on the most important information facts and concepts.
- **Create a visual map.** Also known as a Mind Map, a visual map is a flowchart or diagram of your notes. One way to do it is to place the main topic in the center of the page, with the subtopics and supporting details branching off.

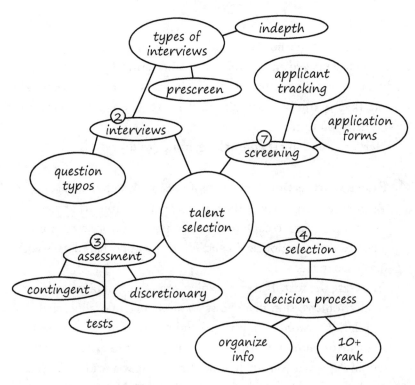

Figure 4.1. Mind Map Example

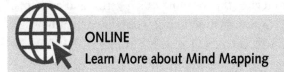

ONLINE
Learn More about Mind Mapping

"Mind Mapping," Student Services Information Desk, The University of Sheffield, https://www.sheffield.ac.uk/ssid/301/study-skills/everyday-skills/mind-mapping

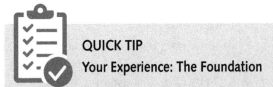

QUICK TIP
Your Experience: The Foundation

You don't start from zero when you begin to prepare for the SHRM certification exam. You have been working in the HR field, perhaps for many years, so you already know a lot about the facts and concepts that will be on the test. Keep your own experience in mind as you study by thinking about how the content you're learning relates to your own experience.

Use flash cards

If you've ever learned a new language, you know that flash cards are an essential learning tool. Flash cards with key questions on the front and the answers on the back are terrific study tools that help you learn and see how well you are retaining what you learn. When you look at the first side of the card, you either know what's on the other side or you don't. If you don't, you'll know to keep working on that fact, term, acronym, or concept.

FMLA	**Family Medical Leave Act**

Figure 4.2. Flash Cards Example

The Leitner System

The Leitner System for using flash cards was developed by Austrian science writer Sebastian Leitner to improve his own ability to retain what he learned. Called "spaced repetition," it's a very powerful technique to help you recall what you study.

Leitner set up a box with several compartments. He put new flash cards in the first compartment and used them every day to test his recall of what he was learning. When he answered a question correctly, he moved the flash card to a second compartment.

Every two days, he tried again to answer the questions on the flash cards in the second compartment. The ones he got right moved to a third compartment, and the ones he got wrong moved back to the first compartment.

Several days later, he tried to answer the questions on the cards in the third compartment. This time, the ones he got wrong moved back to the first compartment and the ones he got right moved to a fourth compartment. As cards moved into "higher" compartments, he tested himself on those topics less and less frequently, focusing instead on the topics he had difficulty recalling.

Tips for using flash cards

- Set up a box like Leitner's with separate compartments or create your own variation with single boxes or rubber bands that separate the levels of cards into packs.
- If you use the SHRM Learning System to help you prepare for the exam, you'll have access to a set of prepared flash cards. These can be viewed online in the product or are available to print at your convenience. Otherwise, you can make your own. When you run across a term, fact, or concept that is new to you, write it on one side of a 3x5 or 4x6 card. Then write the answer or description on the other. In fact, the process of creating your own flash cards can help you learn.
- Carry flash cards with you so you can test yourself while you're standing in line, waiting for an appointment, or have a few minutes of spare time. You'll be surprised by how much studying you do during those "dead" times.

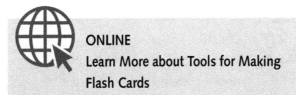

ONLINE
Learn More about Tools for Making
Flash Cards

Put the words "create flash cards" into a web
browser and you'll find a variety of low-cost tools
for making your own.

Be the teacher

A great way to see how well you understand and can recall what you're learning is to explain or teach it to others. Trying to convey facts and information to someone who knows little or nothing about the subject helps you quickly discover what you know well and what you need to work on.

The Feynman Technique

When he was a student at Princeton, Physicist Richard Feynman developed an active recall system that relied heavily on the idea of teaching what he was learning to a child.

The idea is that teaching a child forces you to break down what you're learning and translate it into clear, simple language. You can do that only if you truly understand it. The process helps you remember what you've already learned and discover the gaps in your learning.

You don't have to have a child around to practice this technique. Your "student" can be anyone who is unfamiliar with the subject. Plan a lesson to teach something you're learning to that person. When you use your notes to "teach," you'll quickly discover how well you actually know the material.

ONLINE

Learn More about Active Recall, the Leitner System and the Feynman Technique

"Active Recall is an Effective Learning Technique," *Speak to Your Mind* (blog), July 05, 2016, https://www.speaktoyourmind.com/blog/active-recall

Robert Harris, "Learning Strategy 10: The Leitner Flash Card System," February 27, 2014, https://www.virtualsalt.com/learn10.html

Taylor Pipes, "Learning From the Feynman Technique," *Evernote* (blog), July 21, 2017, https://evernote.com/blog/learning-from-the-feynman-technique/

Study with others

Studying with other learners can be a vital part of the learning process. In fact, researchers have found that people who study together in groups often succeed at a higher rate than students who study alone. Study group members help one another understand the material, review what they are learning, and identify gaps in their learning. They share resources and help one another build confidence as they prepare for the exam.

Study group members typically meet face-to-face, usually once or twice a week. But if there are not enough test-takers for a face-to-face group in your area, you can find or form a virtual group with other HR professionals who are preparing for the same test. Your local SHRM chapter can help.

A coworker and I participated in a group training program through the local SHRM chapter. We both purchased the learning materials and combined [them] with the group sessions [which] provided additional support and interaction that more fully prepared us for the exam.

ONLINE
Find Your Local SHRM Chapter

https://www.shrm.org/search/pages/LocalChapter.aspx

How study groups can help prepare you for answering SJIs

Study groups are particularly helpful to prepare for answering situational judgment items when group members work together to explore critical incidents in their own workplaces.

Here's how: Ask each member to present a critical incident that happened recently at work. For each incident, the group discusses...

- What happened, what HR issues such as compensation, ethics, etc., were involved, and what challenges the incident posed.
- What to consider when addressing the challenges, such as who was involved, time pressures, possible results of action or inaction, etc.
- What the best practice would have been in the given situation.

Tips for making the most of study group time

- Choose group members who are studying for the same test, either the SHRM-CP or SHRM-SCP
- Keep the group to a manageable size—three to five people is ideal
- Have a specific agenda for each meeting that shows the topics to be covered, time allotted for each topic, who will bring what, and so on
- Use assignments to encourage everyone to participate: for example, ask everyone come prepared to explain or teach one topic to the others
- Limit socializing to the first and last five minutes of the meeting
- Schedule regular meetings, and try to schedule them for the same days and times

- Choose a place that is free of distractions and one where you are unlikely to be interrupted
- For each meeting, choose a moderator who will step in as needed to keep the meeting on track and make sure everyone has a chance to participate; if needed, set time limits to keep one person from dominating discussions
- Close each meeting by having everyone mention something they learned
- Before the end of each meeting, set up the agenda and choose the moderator for the next one
- Between meetings, use email or text to ask the other members questions that come up as you study
- After each meeting, list the topics you do not fully know and understand and adjust your study plan as needed

Other study tips

- **Learn from former test-takers.** People who have already earned their SHRM-CP or SHRM-SCP certification can be a great source of tips and advice. Having already gone through the process, they have the advantage of hindsight: what worked and what they wish they'd done differently.
- **Take an exam preparation course.** The SHRM Learning System is available through self-study and instructor-led options. Create a customized learning experience to guide you through practice tests, interactive study tools, and more to help you prepare for the certification exam.
- **Pace yourself and take study breaks.** Studying takes an enormous amount of concentration and energy. Schedule breaks during your study sessions. Stand up and stretch, walk around, or get a snack. But avoid the temptation to distract yourself by checking your phone or email!

> I attended a learning class for eight weeks while using the SHRM Learning System. I spent a lot of time doing the quizzes, flash cards, and scenarios.

- **Make time for yourself.** Taking time away from study—from even thinking about the exam—not only helps you feel better, it keeps you from suffering "information overload." Make time for activities that you enjoy and help you stay healthy. Relax with family and friends. Go for long walks or a run. Go to the gym, take a yoga class, or get a massage. Refreshing yourself helps you feel more relaxed, which in turn helps you concentrate on what you need to learn.

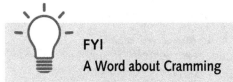

FYI
A Word about Cramming

Cramming is the practice of working furiously to try absorbing a lot of information in a short amount of time, usually just before a test. We've all done it when we've had to take a test for which we haven't really studied. But researchers have found that learners are seldom able recall much information after cramming. Cramming just before a test can be a helpful way to review the material. But it takes dedicated study to learn.

QUICK TIP
Study Best Practices

- Learn actively, not passively
- Read to remember
- Use flash cards
- Be the teacher
- Study with others
- Learn from former test-takers
- Take an exam preparation course
- Pace yourself and take study breaks
- Make time for yourself

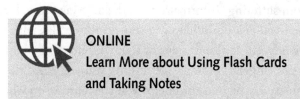

ONLINE
Learn More about Using Flash Cards and Taking Notes

Thomas Frank, "How to Study Effectively with Flash Cards," July 26, 2016, YouTube Video, 8:43, https://www.youtube.com/watch?v=mzCEJVtED0U

Jennifer Gonzalez, "Note-taking: A Research Roundup," Cult of Pedagogy, September 9, 2018, https://www.cultofpedagogy.com/note-taking/

CrashCourse, "Taking Notes: Crash Course Study Skills #1," August 8, 2017, YouTube Video, 8:50, https://www.youtube.com/watch?v=E7CwqNHn_Ns

Chapter 5

Where and When You Study Matters

Your talents and abilities will improve over time, but for that you have to start.

—Martin Luther King

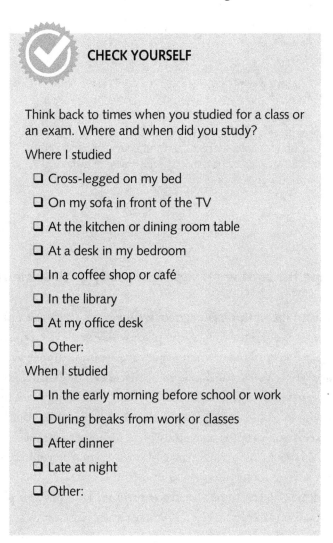

CHECK YOURSELF

Think back to times when you studied for a class or an exam. Where and when did you study?

Where I studied

☐ Cross-legged on my bed

☐ On my sofa in front of the TV

☐ At the kitchen or dining room table

☐ At a desk in my bedroom

☐ In a coffee shop or café

☐ In the library

☐ At my office desk

☐ Other:

When I studied

☐ In the early morning before school or work

☐ During breaks from work or classes

☐ After dinner

☐ Late at night

☐ Other:

Walk into any Starbucks and you'll see people hard at work on laptops or with books and notepads next to their coffee cups. Some people concentrate well when other people are nearby, in front of the TV, late at night, or in brief periods between other activities. But most of us find it easier to focus on work or study in a place that is quiet, comfortable, and free of distractions, when we block out specific times for study, and when we are rested and alert.

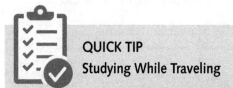

QUICK TIP
Studying While Traveling

If your job involves a lot of travel, you might have to study while on the road, so you'll have to find a quiet place in which you can concentrate. Your hotel room will be private and, hopefully, quiet with few distractions. Most hotels also have quiet public spaces such as conference rooms or quiet lobby areas. If not, ask the desk where to find a library.

Tips for setting up the right study environment

- **Study in the same place regularly.** Once you decide on a place, it becomes "your" study place, the place where you expect to study.
- **Unless you study best when others are around, choose a quiet place where you are unlikely to be disturbed or distracted**—not a busy café, the company cafeteria, your desk during work hours, the sofa in front of the TV, or the kitchen table while your kids are awake. If you can't set up a study place at home, your local library probably has a spot where you can work, or maybe your company has a private room you can use in the off hours.
- **Minimize distractions and interruptions.** Turn off your phone (or leave it somewhere else). If you use the computer to study, turn

off email notification signals. If you're studying in the office or at home while family members or roommates are around, ask everyone not to disturb you. If necessary, put a sign on the door that says, "Working—please don't disturb me!"

- **Make sure you have everything you need.** Set up your study space so you don't have to interrupt yourself to get water to stay hydrated, snacks for extra energy, or coffee if you can't do without it.

- **Make yourself comfortable.** You'll need good light, a comfortable chair, enough room to spread out learning materials, pens or pencils, writing tablets, a laptop if you'll be using it, and so on. Arrange all those things ahead of time so you can focus on learning.

- **Keep a regular study schedule.** Set aside certain hours of each day for study just as you do for meals, sleep, and exercise. Choose a time of day when you'll feel rested and alert. If you work full-time, decide whether you're at your best early in the morning or in the evening. If you have free time during the day, decide whether you're at your best in the mornings or the afternoons. Also consider the times of day when you are least likely to be interrupted.

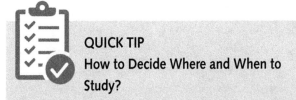

QUICK TIP

How to Decide Where and When to Study?

- Study in the same place regularly.
- Study where you are unlikely to be disturbed or distracted.
- Minimize distractions and interruptions.
- Make sure you have everything you need.
- Make yourself comfortable.
- Keep a regular study schedule.

EXPLORE
Where and When Will You Study?

Where I will study:

_____

_____

When I will study:

_____

_____

Chapter 6
Create a Smart Study Plan

Good luck is when opportunity meets preparation, while bad luck is when lack of preparation meets reality.

—Eliyahu Goldratt

CHECK YOURSELF

Think about a project you have completed. What did you do to get started and make sure you did everything you needed to do to achieve your goals?

_____

_____

_____

_____

Imagine this: you have two weeks of vacation coming up. You've decided to use that time to travel to somewhere you've never been. You're very excited about taking this trip, and you want it to be perfect!

But "perfect" doesn't just happen. Great trips require careful planning. You need to decide where you will go, how you will get there, where you will stay, what you will see and do, what to pack, and more.

With careful planning, you can leave on your trip relaxed and confident that you will have a wonderful time.

"Perfect" doesn't just happen when you prepare for an exam, either. It takes a thoughtfully created study plan, so you can be relaxed and confident on test day. Your study plan will help you:

- Make the best use of the time you have available to study
- Set priorities so you focus on the right work at the right time
- Avoid procrastinating and keep yourself on track

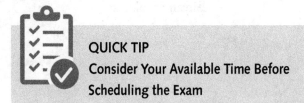

QUICK TIP
Consider Your Available Time Before Scheduling the Exam

To set yourself up for success, consider how much study time you'll have available *before* you schedule the exam. It's better to wait for the next exam window than to try cramming too much study into too little time.

What your study plan should include

A well-designed study plan includes:

I took the pre-test assessment in the Learning System before beginning to study to see where strengths and weaknesses were and then immersed myself in the material for several months.

- Your **goal** for each study session: for example, you might want to be able to list the three most important... describe the best way to ... explain what to do if...
- Your study **schedule**: a calendar showing the dates and times you have set aside for study, including time for study group meetings

- The **content** you will cover during each study session: the topics you will study to achieve your goal for that session
- The **checkpoints** at which you will assess your progress: when you will take practice tests and make any necessary changes to your study plan to fill in your learning gaps

QUICK TIP
Expect the Unexpected

Things happen to throw the most carefully crafted study plan off track. You or a family member might get sick. There might be a crisis at work. It might take longer than you'd thought to learn a particular topic. Leave extra time in your study schedule so you can catch up if you get behind.

How to create your study plan

As we said earlier, the SHRM BoCK is the "blueprint" for both the SHRM-CP and SHRM-SCP exams, as well as for the SHRM Learning System. All the questions on the SHRM certification exam are based on the topics covered in the BoCK.

Thus, the purpose of studying is to close the gaps between what you already know from your experience in the HR field and what you need to know to become certified. That's why your study plan starts with identifying those gaps. Once you know what you need to learn, you can decide how to focus your study time and set up a workable study schedule.

Identify what you need to learn

Start by reading through the BoCK. Use the competency and topic definitions, key concepts and proficiency standard examples to target your study plan. Note the topics and terminology that you are already familiar with from your HR experience and those that are new to you or presented in a new way. Then make yourself a study checklist that shows the terms, facts, and concepts that you need to learn or know more about.

Group together the items on your checklist that you can study together to identify study "blocks." As you sort items into groups, list the related terms and acronyms. Once you've identified your study blocks, you'll have the outline for your study plan.

Set up a realistic study schedule

Your study schedule is a detailed calendar that shows when you will study specific items on your checklist. Here's how to create that schedule:

1. Figure out how many hours you will need to cover everything on your study checklist. Consider factors such as the extent of your HR experience and how quickly you tend to learn.
2. Determine how much of your time is already committed elsewhere. Consider the time you need for family, work, exercise, personal care, and social activities, along with "down time" and time for the unexpected, such as illness or a heavier-than-usual workload.

   Decide how many hours of study time you will have available each week before the exam. If you plan to form or join a study group and/or take an exam prep course, identify how many hours each week you will need for those activities. Then divide the remaining time into study sessions.
3. Determine a specific, achievable goal for each study session and identify the content you will study so you can achieve that goal. Keep in mind that you'll need more study time for some content than for others and build time into your schedule for practice exams, so you can assess what you are learning.

4. Develop a realistic study schedule that shows your study sessions by date and time, the goal for each session, and the content you'll focus on during that session.

5. Create a week-by-week calendar that includes your scheduled activities for each day during your study period. Include time for:

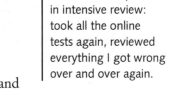

The weeks leading up to the exam I spent in intensive review: took all the online tests again, reviewed everything I got wrong over and over again.

   ◆ Family and friends
   ◆ Work (including your commute)
   ◆ Exercise
   ◆ Study sessions, study group meetings, and exam prep courses (if any)
   ◆ Scheduled appointments (doctors, dentists, etc.)

6. Step back and review your calendar. How realistic is it? Did you leave time for meals and personal care, as well as some "down time" so you can rest and relax? Slack time in case of the unexpected?

QUICK TIP
Learn in "Chunks"

Be careful not to try learning too much during any one session. Researchers have found that studying small "chunks" of content and repeatedly testing yourself on what you've learned helps you remember the information, so you can recall it on exam day.

ONLINE

Kendra Cherry, "How the Chunking Technique Can Help Improve Your Memory," Updated March 30, 2019, https://www.verywellmind.com/chunking-how-can-this-technique-improve-your-memory-2794969

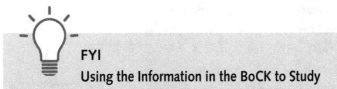

FYI

Using the Information in the BoCK to Study

The Body of Competency and Knowledge (BoCK) provides a thorough go-to resource for framing your study plan and helping you focus on topics that need your attention as you study. An effective way to use the BoCK is to review the following:

- **Behavioral Competencies,** pages 8 and 9 in the BoCK. This section provides an overview of competencies and guidelines on how to read the section; summarizes how the eight behavioral competencies are divided into clusters or related competencies; and provides information on each competency's definition, key concepts, sub-competencies, and proficiency indicators.

- **Drilldown information.** The proficiency indicators for each competency provide example behaviors of what competent behavior "looks like" at two levels—the SHRM-CP (see the "for all HR professionals" column for each competency) and the SHRM-SCP (see the "for Advanced HR professionals" column for each competency).

- **Information about knowledge areas in the three domains—** people, organization and workforce. That information follows the same structure, and the example behaviors appear in the same format as the proficiency indicators for the behavioral competencies.

As you review the BoCK, highlight areas you'd like to include in your study plan. Think through how the behavioral competencies manifest themselves in your daily work in terms of various situations, problems or challenges. Consider how the different behavioral competencies are often used in tandem to resolve issues. For example, communication, global and cultural effectiveness and ethical behavior competencies may all be needed to address a specific issue. Similarly, business acumen, relationship management and consultation may need to be combined to effectively resolve a specific problem.

Use the information in the BoCK to frame your thinking, then use that thinking to inform your study plan. Finally, envision success: Knowledge plus behavior equals success!

CHECK YOURSELF

❑ I have a goal for each study session and have identified the content to cover so I can reach that goal

❑ I have a realistic study schedule that considers my other responsibilities, myself, and the unexpected

❑ I will study at a time of day when I am most rested, alert, and able to concentrate

❑ I have set up a regular, comfortable place to study where I am unlikely to be disturbed or distracted

❑ I will take steps to minimize distractions and interruptions while I am studying

❑ I will make studying a priority

❑ Other:

My study schedule for [week] _____
Test date: _____

Goal: Become proficient in Global and Cultural Effectiveness

Monday	Tuesday	Wednesday	Thursday	Friday	Saturday	Sunday
7:30–9:30 pm	7:30–9:30 pm	7:30–9:30 pm	7:30–9:30 pm	No study	10:00–noon	4:00–6:30 pm
Read Global and Cultural Effectiveness Competency	*Focus*: strategies to develop global mindset; list skills needed for Global HR	*Focus*: culture: definition, layers; theories	*Focus*: obstacles to cross-cultural understanding & strategies to negotiate cultural differences		Meet with study group 3:30–5:30 pm *Focus*: Related terminology	Review and practice

Figure 6.1. Excerpt from Study Plan Calendar

Part Three

Sharpen Your Test-Taking Skills

Believe in yourself! Have faith in your abilities!
Without a humble but reasonable confidence in your
own powers you cannot be successful or happy.

—Norman Vincent Peale

CHECK YOURSELF

Which statements best describe your strategies when you sit down to take a multiple-choice exam? Mark all that apply.

❑ I eliminate responses that obviously don't answer the question

❑ I look for "clues" in the way the question is worded

❑ I consider the order in which the answers appear

❑ If I'm not sure what the answer is, I skip the question

❑ I keep in mind that "None of the above" responses are more likely to be right

❑ If I'm not sure of the answer, I make an educated guess

❑ If an answer says something I know to be true, I assume it's correct

❑ I sometimes think the question isn't asking what I think it's asking—there's some hidden meaning

❑ I keep in mind it pays to overthink the question because it really can't be that straightforward

❑ Other:

There are all kinds of "urban legends" about multiple-choice exams: the exam writers throw in questions to lead you in the wrong direction; the order in which responses appear provide clues about which answer is right; it's better to skip a question than make a wrong guess; a long answer is always more likely to be right than a short answer; the question isn't really asking what it seems to be asking—there's some hidden meaning; it pays to overthink the question because it can't be that straightforward; and more.

None of those statements is true about the SHRM-CP and SHRM-SCP exams. There are no "trick" questions, and there is no "SHRM answer." You will not be given "none of the above" or "all of the above" choices. A response can be true but not necessarily right in the context of the question asked. There might be more than one effective response to questions posed about a situational judgment item based on a scenario, but only one will be *best* in the context presented. The order of the responses has nothing to do with whether a response is correct.

In short, there are no SHRM questions or SHRM answers: SHRM manages the process, but we do not write the questions. All the items on the SHRM exams are written by SHRM-certified HR professionals using the BoCK as their guide, and the questions are rigorously validated to make sure that they accurately measure your HR knowledge. So instead of relying on urban legends, use your reasoning skills, your HR experience, and what you've learned from studying to decide which responses to select.

> I'm not a standardized test fan, so I focused on studying and test-taking skills.

Chapter 7

Understanding the Two Types of Exam Questions

Successful and unsuccessful people do not vary greatly in their abilities. They vary in their desires to reach their potential.

—John Maxwell

As we discussed in the last chapter and elsewhere in this book, the certification exam has two types of test questions: knowledge items and situational judgment items. While both types are multiple-choice questions with four possible responses, there is one important difference between them: There is only one *right* answer to knowledge items, and only one *best* answer to situational judgment items as determined by a panel of your peers—SHRM-certified HR professionals.

Knowledge Items (KIs)

The test includes 95 knowledge and foundational knowledge questions that test the extent of your HR expertise. Knowledge items cover the three knowledge domains of the BoCK: people, organization, and workplace. Foundational knowledge items cover key concepts in the three behavioral competency clusters of the BoCK: leadership, interpersonal and business.

Most of the knowledge items cover topics that are specific to HR professionals, such as talent acquisition, recruiting, and succession planning. The remainder cover topics associated with the eight behavioral

competencies that all professionals need to know, such as ethical practice, communication, and leadership.

There is only *one* correct answer to each knowledge item or foundational knowledge item.

Situational Judgment Items (SJIs)

Sixty-five items on the test are designed to assess your judgment
and decision-making skills in specific HR-related situations. You will
read a scenario and then answer two to four questions that present plausible strategies for addressing issues posed in that scenario. Each question will have four responses that show possible courses of action, from
very ineffective to very effective.

The scenarios for SJIs come directly from HR professionals all over
the world who have shared critical incidents that actually occurred in
their workplaces. Unlike KIs, there is no "right" answer to SJIs—more
than one of the possible responses might be effective in the given situation. But only *one* of the responses will describe the most effective
strategy as determined by the expert judgments of experienced HR
professionals. Your job is to identify that response by determining what
should be done in the situation.

ONLINE
Find More Sample Questions

https://lp.shrm.org/SHRMCertificationPracticeQuestions.html

Myth #1: "Look for the SHRM answer."

Myth #1 debunked: Incorrect. Even though this "advice" appears in many social media discussions, it is absolutely wrong. Do not look for the "SHRM" answer. Why? Because there isn't one! Know your subject matter and don't overthink or read into the questions; just answer the questions being asked.

Myth #2: "Look for clues to the right answer to a knowledge question—often the longest or shortest answer is correct."

Myth #2 debunked: Also wrong. Each SHRM-certified HR subject matter expert must write four plausible response options of approximately the same length. They are specifically told not to write "tricky" questions, so don't look for "clues" like the length of the response. There aren't any.

Myth #3: "I've got a lot of experience, I can 'wing it'—I don't need to prepare."

Myth #3 debunked: Not advisable. Think of a time when you didn't prepare for a major presentation. How did that go? Probably not well. You need to know the subject matter, so leverage the resources you have and create a study plan to help you succeed.

Myth #4: "Situational judgment items scare me; I know I'm not going to do well on those."

Myth #4 debunked: Shift your point of view. Remember that you manage similar situations every day at work. Think about similar challenges you've encountered or problems you've solved—how did you decide which course of action to take in those situations? Think about best practices in HR. All these will help you prepare so you will feel more confident on test day.

Myth #5: "The exam automatically presents successively more difficult questions each time you answer a question correctly."

Myth #5 debunked: Untrue. Dynamic exams present successively more difficult questions after an examinee answers the previous question correctly—but the SHRM exams are not dynamic exams. While there are standardized tests on the market that are dynamic exams, such as the GRE, the SHRM exams are not built this way and are not administered this way. This myth is simply untrue.

Figure 7.1. Dispelling Five Myths about the SHRM Certification Exam

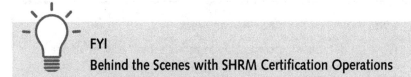

FYI

Behind the Scenes with SHRM Certification Operations

SHRM's BoCK is based on a practice analysis of the HR profession and serves as the basis for the SHRM certification exams. The test blueprint is derived from the BoCK and provides a framework that specifies how many questions to include on each exam from each of the BoCK's 15 HR knowledge areas and 8 behavioral competencies. Two item types comprise the SHRM certification exams: knowledge items and situational judgment items.

Knowledge items are stand-alone multiple-choice items, and each tests a single piece of knowledge or application of knowledge. Knowledge items have only one correct response option, are linked to a specific source and have a rationale that explains why the correct response option is correct and the three other options are incorrect.

In comparison, situational judgment items present realistic situations that are likely to occur in practice and are similar to what many HR professionals have likely experienced during their HR careers. Based on the scenario presented, situational judgment items ask test-takers to consider the problem presented in the question within the context of the situation, and then select the best course of action to take. Like knowledge items, each situational judgment item has four response options from which to choose.

HR professionals provide the "raw materials" for situational judgment items: critical incidents drawn from real-life situations. HR professionals also provide multiple courses of action to take in the situation, with possible actions ranging from very ineffective to very effective. Scoring panels, also composed of seasoned HR professionals, rate the various responses to identify the "best" or "most effective" response. Because the best answer is based on expert judgments, no rationale exists other than the aggregated opinion of the panelists.

Both question types undergo field-testing, meaning each item is included as a non-scored item on an exam to determine its readiness to become a scored test item. If an item passes muster after field testing, it becomes eligible for scoring as part of the operational item pool. If it does not pass muster, the item is retired, meaning it is not eligible to become a scored item or used on a future test.

—Nancy Woolever, SHRM-SCP

Chapter 8

Practice Makes Perfect!

Through practice, gently and gradually we can collect
ourselves and learn how to be more fully with what we do.

—Jack Kornfield

Roger Federer wasn't born a #1 tennis player, and Yo-Yo Ma didn't just pick up a cello one day and start making beautiful music. It takes lots and lots of practice to master a skill.

Test-taking is also a skill that takes practice to develop.

That's why it's important to take at least one practice test to become familiar with the different kinds of questions and the way they are asked. Practicing helps you answer the test questions more quickly and manage the testing time more effectively. Instead of trying to figure out what the test is all about, you can concentrate on recalling what you know so you can choose the right responses.

There are practice questions at the end of this book. If you decide to use the SHRM Learning System to help you prepare for the exam, you'll have access to more than 1,800 practice questions, as well as an online "post-test."

When and how to take practice tests

It's important to choose the right time to start taking practice tests: not when you first start to study, before you've learned anything, but not too close to your testing date, so you'll have time to use the results to improve. If you can, take the practice tests on a computer, because that's the way you'll be tested in the exam room. You'll be able to answer some questions more quickly than others but aim for an average of 1.5 minutes per question.

There are 3 ways to take practice tests:
1. Untimed with access to your learning materials (open book)
2. Timed but still with open book
3. Timed without any learning materials (closed book), as if you were in the test room

QUICK TIP
Practice Timing the Test

When you take the SHRM exam, you'll have four hours to answer 160 questions. That breaks down to an average of 1.5 minutes per question. You'll be able to answer some questions much more quickly, leaving time for those you find more difficult. Timing yourself when you practice will help you develop a sense of how long it takes to answer both easy and difficult questions.

How to get the most out of practice tests

- Figure out why you incorrectly answered a question, so you can pinpoint what you need to study. Did you get a fact or some terminology wrong? Did you not read a scenario carefully enough?
- What questions were you unsure of? Where did you have to guess? Feeling uncertain about which answer to select could indicate that you don't know that topic as well as you should.
- If possible, take as many different tests as you can.

- When you take timed, closed-book tests, resist the temptation to sneak glances at your learning materials. Put them away and take the test as if it were the real thing.
- Create your own practice tests. Write questions for topics that you don't fully know or understand. Put the "test" aside while you study those topics. Then try to answer the questions.

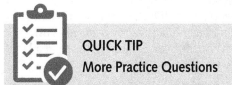

QUICK TIP
More Practice Questions

The SHRM Learning System has over 1,800 practice questions.

ONLINE
Take a Practice Test

Take the online practice test for an experience in answering the types of questions you'll find on the certification exam: https://lp.shrm.org/SHRM CertificationPracticeQuestions.html

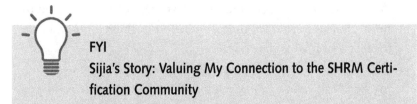

FYI
Sijia's Story: Valuing My Connection to the SHRM Certification Community

Professors and colleagues always cited SHRM as a trustworthy and resourceful HR community, so when I decided to become a certified practitioner, I chose to take the SHRM-CP exam. Now that I am a credential-holder, people from the U.S. and other countries see those letters after my name and admire my achievement. For me, the true value of SHRM certification is finding myself in a larger community and the sense of belonging.

Preparing for the SHRM-CP exam took me back to my time in graduate school, when I was also reading, doing research and sharing views with other students. The SHRM Body of Competency and Knowledge was a well-developed structure within which I could holistically strengthen my academic HR knowledge, as well as apply that knowledge to real-world client cases. Often during my exam prep, I found inspiring answers to client issues.

Support in My Career as a Consultant

I continue to find the SHRM competencies helpful in my work as a young professional in a big consulting firm in China. More company management teams are accepting the competency concept, which in turn (and more importantly) inspires HR practitioners to adopt the right skill sets for facing new challenges. Technical competencies are required by the job, but behavioral competencies enable HR professionals to become true business partners and create value for the organization.

The *Business Acumen* competency, for example, echoed recently throughout a client project involving HR transformation. My team facilitated a shift in mindset from responding to business requests to proactively thinking about business needs and providing services that deliver people-oriented value. That mindset shift was supported by my ability to understand the organization's strategy, operations and external environments, the essence of business acumen.

With my SHRM-CP credential, I have gained the trust of clients looking for a consultant with global insights and a solid understanding of people and organizations. My proficiency in HR knowledge areas and the *Global & Cultural Effectiveness* competency played a role in another recent project for a client that wanted to improve its employee experience across several geographic regions. I was able to help raise the client's awareness of the cultural and mindset differences between its regional leaders (who were mostly from the West) and local staff (who were located in countries across Asia that had quite different cultures and religions, despite being neighbors). The client was then able to place further emphasis on diversity in assessing the project's current status and in planning appropriate initiatives.

Recertification and Enriching HR Knowledge

Study never ends, even after one passes the certification exam.

I use my free time, usually while traveling to and from the office or clients' offices, to read SHRM's *HR Magazine* and newsletters and catch up with popular topics across industries. I also learn from the stories of other SHRM credential-holders to see how I might further elevate my career. At work, the SHRM website is the first resource I go to for insights and practice aids and what I recommend to colleagues and clients. The SHRM Connect online community is where HR peers discuss real issues we encounter daily, express diverse ideas and debate possible solutions. I find the conversations inspiring, as they expose me to cases in the corporate world—a perfect supplement to my work in the consultancy world.

It was most exciting to be invited to join in SHRM-CP test-development activities and to work virtually with a diverse team. Since 2017 I have participated in several rounds of technical review, content validation, bias and cultural sensitivity review, and other important activities, which help to maintain a consistent and high standard for upcoming tests. Completing my assignments and submitting them on time are part of my commitment to HR professionalism.

When I lived in the Washington, D.C., area, I saw the SHRM headquarters building in nearby Alexandria, Va., as a symbol of knowledge. Now, as a SHRM member living on the other side of the Pacific Ocean, each WebEx meeting is a great opportunity for me to feel more connected to the larger community of SHRM-CP credential-holders.

—Sijia Bu, SHRM-CP

Chapter 9
Test-Taking Tips

Being aware of your fear is smart. Overcoming it is the mark of a successful person.

—Seth Godin

The questions on the SHRM certification exam are designed to assess your expertise as an HR professional. As said earlier, each question has been thoroughly vetted by experts in the field, and there are no "trick" questions. But there are strategies that can help you decide which of the four possible answers to choose.

Test-Taking Strategies

- Read the questions and answer choices carefully before making your selection
- Narrow down your choices by eliminating responses that are clearly wrong
- Trust your first impressions
- Don't assume an answer is correct just because its true
- Use your time wisely
- Once you've answered a question, move on
- If you can't answer a question, make an educated guess
- Stay calm

Read carefully before choosing an answer

The way you read the questions and answer choices before responding can make a significant difference in the results. When you skim instead of reading, you might misunderstand the question or miss something important and then choose a response that doesn't really answer the question.

For that reason, be sure to read the *entire* question and *all* the answer choices carefully. For example, if a question asks for a program, make sure your answer is a program. Similarly, if the question asks for a strategy, approach, or method, make sure the answer is a strategy, approach or method.

Read the question first, then answer the question that's being asked

Read the question before you read the answer choices. For long questions, jotting down key words and phrases can help you make sure you understand what the question is asking and keep it in mind when you read the answers.

> The best advice I received was to focus less on figuring out "right" or "wrong" answers and concentrate more on letting my experience guide responses—to take a deep breath and say "how would I solve this problem?"

Once you've read the question, try to predict the answer. For example, if you read the question and think, "X is the right method," look for that method among the answer choices.

But be sure to read *all* the answer choices before you respond. Don't stop at the first one you think is right. It may be a partial answer, and you might find a more correct answer among the other choices.

For situational judgment items, read the scenario before reading the questions

There will be two to four questions about each scenario. Read the scenario first, jotting down key points as you read. Then read and answer the questions one at a time.

Narrow down the choices

After you read the entire question and all the answers you might feel confident that only one of the answers is right. If so, select it and move on. But if you're not sure, use the strikeout feature on the test computer to eliminate any responses that you are certain don't answer the question, are incorrect, or don't make sense in the context. That way, you can focus on the answers that are most likely to be right.

Avoid analyzing what the question *meant* to ask

As we said earlier, first read the question and then answer the question being asked. You can waste a lot of time overthinking questions, especially SJIs. Keep in mind that all you have is the information given in the question. Take it at face value. While in real life, there might be different factors to consider or different ways to approach a situation, your job is to answer the specific question being asked. Do not overthink it or try to read into it; just answer the question that's presented.

Trust your first impression

When you read the answer choices, you are likely to sense that one answer is right. Trust those first impressions. Don't go against that first impulse and change your answer unless you are certain that you were wrong.

Don't assume an answer is right just because it's true

It's easy to assume a statement you know to be true is the answer you should choose. But while an answer choice might be true in another context, it might not be the right answer to the

Don't second-guess yourself! If you read the question and while reading the options one stands out and you feel it is right, it probably is! I strongly believe this is why I passed the exam. I never changed an answer after choosing one and always went with my gut.

question that's being asked. Be sure to read the question and then select the response that best answers that specific question.

Use your time wisely

The certification exam is a timed exam, but it's not a speed test. There is no need to rush. The test is designed so that you have enough time to answer all the questions. But if you forget to check the time or spend too much time on one question, the time could run out before you've been able to answer all the questions. Don't "watch the clock" but do periodically spot-check your time remaining.

That's where your experience and study come in. The more you know about the topics, the more confident you'll feel that you can answer all the questions within the allotted time.

Once you've answered a question, move on

You can waste a lot of time on a single question by second-guessing yourself ("maybe that's not right.") If you're not sure about an answer, flag the question for review and move on to the next. Remember that if you've studied well and read both the question and the answer choices carefully, the odds are good that you'll choose the right answer the first time. Resist the urge to change an answer unless you are 100% sure it's wrong.

I was anxious, very anxious, but by the time I finally got 80% on the online practice test I comforted myself with the knowledge that the value that I was getting was in the learning, and that the test was just a formality. Even if I didn't pass it, I was still going to be a much better HR representative.

If you can't answer a question, guess

No matter how well prepared you are, some questions are bound to stump you. Don't panic, and don't waste time going over and over the question and answer choices. Remember that you will receive credit for all the correct answers and will not be penalized if an answer is wrong.

If you guess when you absolutely don't know the answer, you at least have a 25 percent chance of getting it right—more if you've eliminated the obviously wrong answers first. So strike out the obviously wrong responses, make an educated guess, flag the question for review, and move on.

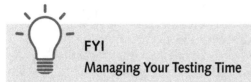

FYI
Managing Your Testing Time

Before I took the SHRM exam, I thought that 4 hours would be a lot of time. I was surprised it went by so quickly! It's very important not to waste any of that time.

Don't spend too much time reading and re-reading a single question. If you find a question confusing, remember that the test isn't trying to trip you up. Relax your brain, choose what seems to be the best answer, mark the question for review, and move on. Once you've reached the end of the test, you can go back and take another look.

The testing timer keeps counting down when you leave the room for a break. Minimize the need for breaks by eating a light meal and not drinking too much water, tea, or coffee. But if the need for a break is making it hard to focus, take one quickly, then come back and pick up where you left off. And if you're pretty sure you will need a break, take one halfway through the test so you'll know you have a lot of time left.

Practice focusing for a 4-hour block of time, so you'll know what that feels like when you take the exam. If you use the SHRM Learning System to help you prepare, you can practice by taking a timed 4-hour test. Otherwise, you can practice by setting aside an uninterrupted 4-hour study session.

—Eddice Douglas, SHRM-CP, Senior Specialist, Education Products

QUICK TIP
Time Saver

Don't waste precious time looking for clues that aren't there. The length of an answer or whether it is A, B, C, or D doesn't give you a clue about which answer is correct, and there are no patterns in the response options. Read each question carefully and choose the response that is the best answer to that question.

Review flagged questions

Once you've answered all the questions, go back to the ones you've marked for review. But first, take a moment or two to stretch or stand up, drink some water, or take a break if you need one. Then go back to the marked items. Just as before, be careful not to spend too much time on a single question, second guess yourself, or change answers unless you're certain you answered it wrong in the first place.

Stay calm

Even if you feel confident that you are ready for the test, you might suddenly find yourself feeling panicky or rushed, and that can lead you to make mistakes. If you feel yourself getting shaky or tense, sit back for a moment and take several deep breaths to calm yourself.

ONLINE
Learn More about SHRM's Certification
Community

Check out the SHRM Community for more test-taking tips and advice: https://community.Shrm.org/home

EXPLORE

Which test-taking strategies do you think will be most useful to you?

_____

_____

_____

Part Four

Managing Test Anxiety

Chapter 10

Recognizing the Symptoms of Anxiety

Smile, breathe, and go slowly.

—Thich Nhat Hanh

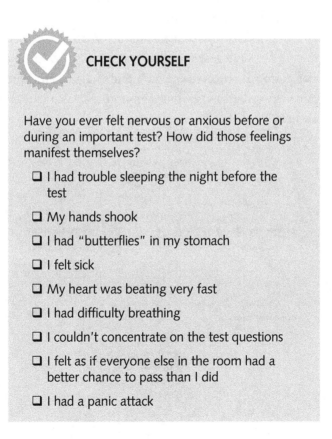

CHECK YOURSELF

Have you ever felt nervous or anxious before or during an important test? How did those feelings manifest themselves?

- ❏ I had trouble sleeping the night before the test
- ❏ My hands shook
- ❏ I had "butterflies" in my stomach
- ❏ I felt sick
- ❏ My heart was beating very fast
- ❏ I had difficulty breathing
- ❏ I couldn't concentrate on the test questions
- ❏ I felt as if everyone else in the room had a better chance to pass than I did
- ❏ I had a panic attack

If you've ever felt nervous or anxious before or during a test, you're not alone. Taking a test is a form of performance, and performers of all kinds, from professional actors and musicians to conference presenters often feel the symptoms of performance anxiety, or "stage fright."

Even though you don't have to stand up in front of people to take a professional test like the SHRM exam, you are being asked to demonstrate what you know. It's not uncommon for test-takers to worry that they won't be able to perform well. The higher the stakes, the greater the anxiety.

In fact, a little performance anxiety can be a good thing. It can increase your focus and concentration, helping you to do your best. But for some people, anxiety can lead to feelings of panic that result in what they most fear: failure.

> Feeling anxious made me more focused on the test and test preparation managed my anxiety and made me feel more excited to achieve a valuable certificate.

The good news is that most test-takers experience only mild symptoms that they can manage easily by understanding what causes their anxiety and learning how to reduce it. Even if you have a history of performance anxiety, you'll find that the strategies in this section can help you manage your symptoms, so you can focus your attention where it belongs: on the exam.

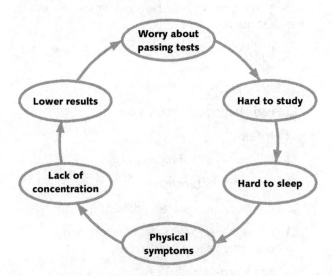

Figure 10.1. The Test Anxiety Cycle

The symptoms of test anxiety

Test anxiety manifests itself in a variety of ways. The symptoms can vary considerably and range from mild to severe.

Most of us have felt at least some of these symptoms at one time or another. You can't concentrate, and your mind races with negative thoughts: "I'll never be able to do this." "I'm not good enough." "I'm going to fail." You have trouble sleeping. You have "butterflies" in your stomach and feel a little nauseous; your mouth is dry, and your hands are sweaty and shaking; your heart races.

Those symptoms have a physical basis: they come from what psychologists call the "fight or flight response." When faced by a real or imaginary threat, the body releases adrenaline to prepare itself to either fight or run away from the threat. That was very useful when we were threatened by predators in the wild. It's not so helpful to us today.

Test anxiety can also create a type of "noise" in your brain that makes it difficult to recall information from your memory. That noise can make it hard to understand test questions and make reasoned judgments about which responses to select.

Where test anxiety comes from

Why do some people experience little test anxiety, while others have so much anxiety they can hardly get through an exam? Here is some of what researchers found when they set out to find the sources of test anxiety.

- **Parents' expectations and extent of parental support.** All parents have certain expectations for their children: they want their kids to be happy and do well. But you might feel more test anxiety when you're faced with a challenge if your parents had very high or unreasonable expectations for your achievement, and/or gave you little emotional support when you faced difficult situations as a child.

- **Schools' increased reliance on testing.** Even though it's been a long time since you were in elementary and high school, your early learning experiences can affect the way you feel about tests. For example, you might continue to feel anxious about tests well into adulthood if your teachers focused more on testing than on learning and pressured you to do well on tests for which you were not adequately prepared.
- **A fear of failure.** Test anxiety is a fear of not performing well, and it's normal to feel some level of performance anxiety. You might experience much higher levels if you lack confidence or have very high standards for yourself and care a lot about what people think of you.
- **A history of performing poorly on tests.** It's a vicious cycle: you don't usually do well on tests, so you think you can't do well on tests, and, as a result, you actually don't do well on tests.
- **Being unprepared.** There's no doubt about it: Taking a high-stakes exam when you haven't prepared is a sure-fire recipe for anxiety.

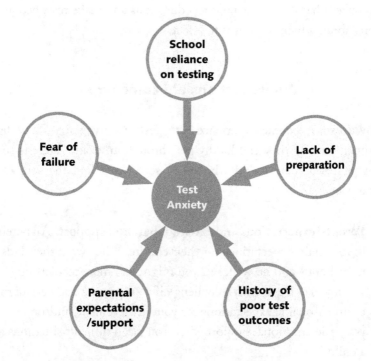

Figure 10.2. Sources of Test Anxiety

FYI
Tough Love

There is no replacement for preparation. Accept this tough love or convert it into a simple truth that applies only to you!

Know your stuff. Think about any exam you've ever taken; think about how important it is to know the subject matter. This exam is no different—you have to know your subject matter.

You must prepare. Have you ever improvised at the last minute or run out of time to properly prepare for a major presentation? Think about how well or how badly that situation turned out for you. A certification exam is a serious undertaking and preparing to take the exam is crucial. Don't try to wing it!

Don't wait until the last minute. Invest in yourself by setting aside the time to adequately prepare. Try not to *overprepare* but do make sure you are comfortable with the subjects that might be tested on the exam, and make sure you allow yourself time to reflect on your work experiences. Thinking through and jotting down bullet points about situations you've encountered and managed at work will help you think through the situations presented on the exam.

Envision success. Picture this: you finish the exam, and a notice appears that states "Congratulations. You passed." Envision succeeding and establish a roadmap to lead you to success. Plan well, prepare for your exam experience. And when you get to the test center, take a deep breath. Leveraging exam-preparation strategies can help you focus and dispel anxieties.

Good luck on the exam!

—Nancy Woolever, SHRM-SCP

QUICK TIP
Anxiety Reappraisal

Some researchers, including Alison Wood Brooks from the Harvard Business School, have found that some anxiety can actually improve performance. The theory is that anxiety and excitement are similar kinds of emotions and reframing anxiety as excitement can change your mindset from "threat" to "opportunity." https://www.theatlantic.com /health/archive/2014/01/study-fight-performance -anxiety-by-getting-excited/282886/

Chapter 11
Strategies for Reducing Anxiety

Before anything else, preparation is the key to success.

—Alexander Graham Bell

Test anxiety can come on unexpectedly, even for people with little history of nervousness about tests. That's especially true when the stakes are high, and success is very important. Luckily, there are steps you can take to keep anxiety from getting in the way of your performance on the certification exam.

Build your confidence by preparing thoroughly

Imagine that a colleague has asked you to step in at the last minute to give an important talk. You're familiar with the topic, but you don't know it well, and there isn't any time to learn more. All you have going into the presentation room are the slides and notes that your colleague handed you an hour earlier.

How confident do you think you'd feel that you could do a good job of delivering the presentation? Chances are that you'd not feel very confident at all. It would be no surprise if your hands shook, your mouth got dry, and your mind went blank as soon as you stood up in front of the group.

To deliver the presentation with confidence, you would need to very good grasp of the subject matter. The better your understanding of the topic, the more likely it would be that you'd be able to make a great presentation.

I wanted this certification so badly, I really made it my second priority next to my day job. I took vacation days to study, which helped reduce my anxiety as the time approached. I also made sure I got enough sleep and exercise.

It's the same with taking the certification exam. The better you know and understand the material, the more confident you'll feel that you'll be able to pass. That confidence makes it far less likely that you would experience the high levels of anxiety that could get in the way of your success.

Practice realistic thinking

The anxious mind is a very busy mind, and not in a good way. Test anxiety brings with it lots of negative thoughts that make it hard to think clearly.

But consider this: *thinking* something doesn't mean it's real. *Thinking* that you can't possibly pass the exam doesn't mean you are ordained to fail.

When those negative thoughts start ricocheting around in your brain, take a step back and examine them. *Why* is the test too hard for you? *Why* won't you be able to pass? *How* do you know you can't do well?

Once you've looked at the negative thoughts more objectively, remind yourself that you have worked hard to prepare yourself for success. Every time a negative thought comes up, look at it realistically and tell yourself, "Yes, it's a challenging exam, but I'm ready to do my very best!"

Keep a journal

One proven way to help manage anxiety is to write down what you're thinking and feeling as test day approaches. Researchers have learned that writing about stressful events can improve your ability to learn, solve problems, and more. Some have found that "expressive writing" has an effect on the capacity of your working memory.

Buy a notebook and carry it with you, use the "Notes" app on your phone, or download a journaling app. Find a quiet place a few times to day to jot down what you're thinking and feeling as test day approaches. When you find yourself thinking negative thoughts, write them down and then ask, "Why am I feeling this way?" Write down your realistic thoughts: "I feel confident that I'm preparing well enough to succeed on this test." "This is going to be hard, but I can do it."

Learn how to calm yourself

Even if you've prepared thoroughly and feel confident that you know the material, you might suddenly feel nervous or anxious before or during the exam. Learning how to calm yourself can help you concentrate. Don't wait for test day to try these techniques; practice them early so you can access them when you need them.

- **Slow and deepen your breathing.** When you're under stress, you might notice that you are taking rapid, shallow breaths, which can make you feel even more tense. Learn to calm your breathing. Take several slow, deep breaths and let them out easily and smoothly. Keep your attention focused on your breathing. Try to "watch" the air move in and out of your body.
- **Tense, then relax your muscles.** Tightness in the shoulders and other muscle groups are a common response to stress. Practice relaxing your body. One by one, tighten specific muscle groups, then slowly release them on a long out breath. For example, shrug your shoulders up to your ears on an in breath and let them down slowly on an out breath. Gently roll your head from side to side and around in circles. If you do these kinds of exercises a few times daily, you'll be able to draw on them more easily if you start to feel tense in the exam room.
- **Visualize.** Find a quiet place and close your eyes. Visualize yourself walking into the test room, sitting down at the computer, and taking the test. See yourself finishing the test, knowing that you've done well. Hold a picture in your mind of yourself holding your SHRM certificate.

- **Participate in activities that help you shake off stress.** Studying for the exam is an intense process, and it can be helpful to do things that help you feel calmer and less stressed. You might take a yoga or a meditation class, get massages, work out at the gym, or take long walks. Those kinds of activities can get you out of your mind and help you learn to relax.

Be ready for test day

You're unlikely to feel relaxed if you've spent all night before the test studying and rush to get to the testing center on time. Set aside some time for review the day before the test. Then get a good night's rest and eat a good meal before you leave for the test center.

> I felt anxiety throughout my studying, but the day before the exam I took off from work and just relaxed—no studying. On test day I didn't feel anxious at all.

Make sure you know how to get to the test center, and plan to get there early so you don't feel rushed. When you arrive, greet some of the other test-takers. Preview the navigation functions on the exam computer so you'll be familiar with them when the test starts.

If you feel nervous or tense as the test starts, use your breathing and relaxation techniques to calm yourself down.

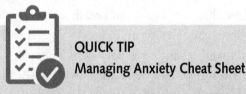

QUICK TIP
Managing Anxiety Cheat Sheet

- Understand the reasons for test anxiety
- Prepare thoroughly
- Practice realistic thinking
- Keep a journal
- Learn how to calm yourself
- Be ready for test day

ONLINE
Learn More about
Managing Test Anxiety

Sian Leah Beilock, "Why We Choke Under Pressure—and How to Avoid It," Filmed November 2017, TEDMED 2017 video, 15:14, https://www.ted.com/talks/sian_leah_beilock_why_we_choke_under_pressure_and_how_to_avoid_it.

"Overcoming Test Anxiety," Office of Academic Support & Counseling, Albert Einstein College of Medicine, https://www.einstein.yu.edu/education/student-affairs/academic-support-counseling/medical-school-challenges/test-anxiety.aspx

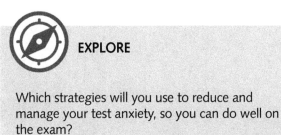

EXPLORE

Which strategies will you use to reduce and manage your test anxiety, so you can do well on the exam?

_____

_____

_____

Chapter 12

The Perils of Procrastination

The secret of getting ahead is getting started.

— Mark Twain

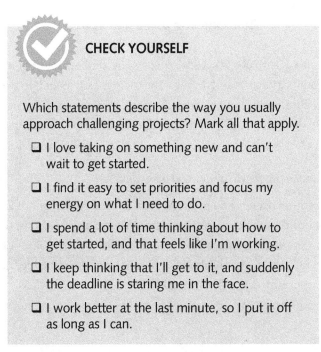

CHECK YOURSELF

Which statements describe the way you usually approach challenging projects? Mark all that apply.

❏ I love taking on something new and can't wait to get started.

❏ I find it easy to set priorities and focus my energy on what I need to do.

❏ I spend a lot of time thinking about how to get started, and that feels like I'm working.

❏ I keep thinking that I'll get to it, and suddenly the deadline is staring me in the face.

❏ I work better at the last minute, so I put it off as long as I can.

"I don't have enough time now—I'll get to this later."
"I've still got a couple of weeks and I work better under pressure."
"I'm not in the mood right now."
"I work better under pressure."

Sound familiar? Those are the words of a typical procrastinator. Most of us procrastinate once in a while. But in the end, we usually pull ourselves together and get the work done.

But for some people, procrastination is a life-long problem. They've always left things until the very last minute, pulling all-nighters before a paper or a report is due, cramming for tests, and struggling to meet deadlines. Even though they usually manage to get by, there's a cost: diminished performance and increased anxiety.

The good news is that there are proven ways to manage any tendency toward procrastination that you might have. The first step is to understand that procrastinating isn't being lazy. Researchers have discovered a lot about why people procrastinate.

Reasons for procrastination

Looked at objectively, it's easy to see that procrastinating makes no sense. Your rational mind knows that you need to get to work, but you keep finding ways to distract yourself even when delaying is obviously self-defeating. Understanding the reasons for procrastination can help you change your behavior, so you can accomplish your goals.

People procrastinate when they feel overwhelmed

Imagine you've been asked to move your entire department of 25 people to a new building. Where do you start? What do you need to do?

Big, important projects like that can be overwhelming. "There's so much to do," you might think. "It's too much for me to tackle." Studying for an important exam like the SHRM-CP or the SHRM-SCP can feel the same way.

What to do

To tackle any big project, break it down into a series of manageable tasks—it's much easier to do a series of tasks than to try doing everything at once. In fact, that's the purpose of your study plan.

Your study plan is like the detailed plan a contractor follows to build the home shown in the architect's blueprints. It includes specific goals, action steps for achieving them, and a timetable for taking each action. Breaking down the process into manageable units makes the whole thing less daunting.

People procrastinate when they have trouble managing their time

We're all so busy these days that there never seems to be enough time. Things always take longer than we expect, and our to-do lists just keep on growing. It can be a major challenge even to think about finding the time to study.

I didn't study each night like I should have! Had I studied every night, I do not think the test would have been so stressful and I would not have had to cram in so much reading at the last minute. While I did pass the exam, I can be a testament to future classes that you really do need to study each night—and starting early is the way to go!

What to do

One thing is certain: You can't make more time. What you can do is spend that time more wisely. But first you need to know more about what you are doing with your time. It's like developing a budget: Before you can decide how to use your money, you need to know your current spending patterns.

That's where a time log comes in. A time log helps you track the way you spend your time, so you can manage it more effectively.

Use a columnar tablet, a spreadsheet or an app on your phone to set up your time log. Then track all your activity in 10- or 15-minute increments for at least a week. Include time at work, time getting to and from work, time with family, time watching TV, time exercising, cooking, eating, taking kids to school, posting and checking out your friends on social media, socializing, going to movies, reading on the sofa... just about everything.

Your time log will help you become aware of how you really use your time. You might notice that a task that felt as if it took a couple of hours actually took less than an hour to complete. You might be spending several hours a week doing things that don't really need to be done, or that could be done more efficiently. Seeing how you actually use your time will help you set priorities, so you can free up the time you need for study.

Table 12.1. Time Log Example

DAY & DATE: Thursday, March 6

TIME	ACTIVITY	DURATION	NOTES
6 :30 a.m.	Shower, breakfast, get ready for work	1 hour	
7:30 a.m.	Commute to work	1 hour	Heavy traffic, no spaces in parking lot
8:30 a.m.	Check and answer email	15 minutes	
8:45 a.m.	Prepare for weekly meeting	30 minutes	
9:15 a.m.	Ran into Sam on way to bathroom, chatted about his new baby	15 minutes	
9:30 a.m.	Read Redfin notification re interesting new home listing & called Pat	10 minutes	
9:40 a.m.	Looked for copy of job descriptions posted last month	15 minutes	Couldn't find—finally sent email to Millie
9:55 a.m.	Went down to cafeteria for coffee	10 minutes	
10:05 a.m.	Phone call from James re problem with vacation schedules	15 minutes	3rd call this week
10:20	Set up conference room for weekly meeting	10 minutes	Filling in for Filipe
10:30	Weekly meeting	45 minutes	Dennis late so meeting went long
11:15	Fire alarm went off—building evacuated	1 hour	False alarm (luckily)
12:15	Lunch	45 minutes	Short lunch b/cause of alarm

People might procrastinate because they are afraid of failure—or of success

A common reason for procrastinating is the fear of failing. Why try if you can't succeed? If you don't try, you can rationalize your failure: "If I'd given this project my all, it would have been great."

It's the same with studying for an exam. Why study if you think you have no chance of passing? After all, if you don't study, you can tell yourself: "I could have passed if only I'd had the time to study."

Surprisingly, some people procrastinate because they are afraid of success. Success can bring new challenges, with higher performance expectations, more pressure, and more stress, and that can be scary. It can feel easier not to put in the effort in the first place.

A related reason for procrastination is the fear of not doing something perfectly. Achieving perfection is like trying to scale a wall that gets higher and higher as you climb. If you feel that there's no way to get over the top, why bother?

What to do

Become aware of your fears and the ways in which they obstruct the path toward your goals. Remember that both failures and successes are opportunities to learn and grow.

Instead of worrying about the bad things that could happen if you fail—or succeed—in passing the certification exam, focus on why certification is important to you. Think about the ways in which being certified will benefit you in your career as an HR professional. The more certain you are about the value of passing the test, the easier it will be to make studying for it a priority.

People procrastinate because it's become a habit

Experienced procrastinators have honed the fine art of distracting themselves. Instead of working, they check their phones and email, think about what to have for dinner, find someone to chat with, rearrange their work space, browse the web, clean out the refrigerator, or do myriad other time-wasting things. Then they look up at the clock and wonder where all the time has gone.

What to do

Stopping the procrastinating habit is like stopping smoking: it takes a determined effort.

Try this: write down all the ways in which you distract yourself while you are working or studying. Post the list prominently in your workspace or study space and add to it if you find a new distraction.

When you begin a study session, remove the obvious distractors such as your phone and internet access. Make yourself comfortable with water, coffee, or a snack close at hand if you think you'll need them. Every time you notice yourself thinking about or doing things other than studying, stop for a moment, take a deep breath, remind yourself of how important it is to achieve your goals, and then turn your attention back to your study plan.

Breaking a bad habit can also be easier when you reward yourself for your accomplishments. Give yourself a reward when you reach milestones on your study plan: Indulge in a favorite snack, take a long walk, visit with friends or do something fun with your kids. Get a massage or spend an hour doing absolutely nothing. Put $5 a week into a "rewards" jar to spend once you've reached your final goal: taking the certification exam!

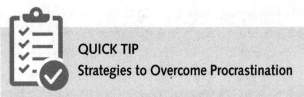

QUICK TIP
Strategies to Overcome Procrastination

- Determine why you procrastinate
- Break projects into manageable tasks or "chunks"
- Learn to manage your time
- Remove distractors
- Focus on what you want to achieve
- Reward yourself for your achievements

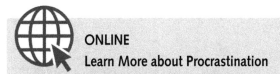

ONLINE

Learn More about Procrastination

Ana Swanson, "The Real Reasons You Procrastinate — and How to Stop," *Washington Post*, April 27, 2016, https://www.washingtonpost .com/news/wonk/wp/2016/04/27/why-you-cant -help-read-this-article-about-procrastination -instead-of-doing-your-job/

Chris Bailey, "5 Research-Based Strategies for Overcoming Procrastination," *Harvard Business Review*, October 4, 2017, https://hbr.org /2017/10/5-research-based-strategies-for -overcoming-procrastination

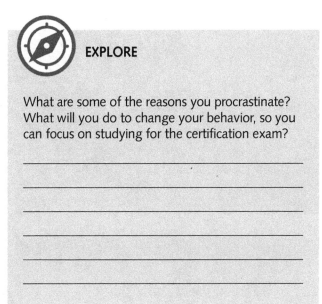

EXPLORE

What are some of the reasons you procrastinate? What will you do to change your behavior, so you can focus on studying for the certification exam?

_____

_____

_____

_____

_____

_____

Part Five

Preparing for Exam Day

Chapter 13

What to Expect on Exam Day

*Success depends upon previous preparation, and
without such preparation there is sure to be failure.*

—Confucius

You've worked very hard to prepare for the certification exam, and now the big day is almost here. Knowing what to expect at the test center can help you feel more comfortable and less nervous.

About the testing center

Your SHRM certification exams will be held at one of Prometric's highly secure testing centers. Prometric operates hundreds of test centers in more than 180 countries, typically in secure testing centers located in office buildings and on college campuses.

Get to the test center early

It's essential to arrive at the test center on time. The test administrator can deny access to late-comers. If that happens, you'll need to re-apply for the exam and pay another fee.

Schedule your time so you will arrive at the test center at least 30 minutes early so you can settle in and be ready to go when the exam starts. It's a good idea to do a "dry run" a few days before the exam: drive or take public transportation to the test center and make a note of how long it takes you. If you'll be driving, figure out where to park.

Then leave extra time in case traffic is heavy or public transit is slow on test day.

Rescheduling the exam

If you can't make your original test date, you can reschedule the exam. There's no charge if you reschedule within the same testing window at least 30 days before the test date. Prometric charges a fee if you need to reschedule less than 30 days before the test date. If you cancel less than 5 days before the test, you will forfeit the fees and need to reapply for another exam window.

In cases of extreme weather or a national emergency, Prometric may need to cancel the exam. In that case, Prometric will reschedule you as soon as possible, and you won't be charged a fee for rescheduling.

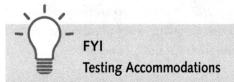

FYI
Testing Accommodations

SHRM and Prometric are fully committed to providing reasonable accommodations for any medical condition that constitutes a qualifying disability under the Americans with Disabilities Act (ADA). See the 2019 *Certification Handbook* for details. https://lp.shrm .org/Certification-Handbook.html?_ga=2.264419084.229982936 .1549558160-1918200587.1540558773

Arriving at the test center

When you arrive at the test center, the test center administrator (TCA) will check you in. The TCA will ask you to show a valid photo identification (ID) and sign a logbook. Be sure you re-read your Authorization to Test letter and review the Prometric website about acceptable forms of ID. Your photo ID must be current, so check it far in advance of your test date in case it is getting ready to expire.

Table 13.1. Rescheduling Exam Appointments

Time Frame	Reschedule Permitted	Stipulations
Requests submitted 30 days or more before original appointment	Yes	None
Requests submitted 5 to 29 days before original appointment	Yes	Candidate must pay Prometric a cancellation fee of $53.00
Requests submitted less than 5 days before original appointment	No	Candidate is considered a "no-show," will forfeit all fees, and will have to reapply and pay the fees for a future exam window.

You can expect a high level of security (not unlike the security you encounter at an airport these days). Bring only what you need into the testing center because you'll need to leave *all* your personal belongings **except** your ID, eyeglasses, and locker key in a locker. That includes your phone and any jewelry except wedding and engagement rings. The TCA will provide note paper and pen or pencil or dry erase board and markers so you can make notes during the test.

Before you enter the testing room, the TCA inspect will inspect your eyeglasses, hair clips, ties, and any other accessories to look for camera devices that could be used to capture exam content. It's a good idea to leave such items as ornate clips, combs, barrettes, headbands, tie clips, and cuff links behind because you might not be allowed to wear them into the testing room. The TCA might ask you to turn out your pockets, and you might also be "wanded" or asked to go through a metal detector.

Although these inspections are thorough, they take only a few seconds. **They will be repeated when you return from breaks** to ensure you do not violate any security protocol.

I followed advice from other test takers who passed, and I did not study the day before the exam. This is challenging to do, but it is very helpful to reduce stress and anxiety.

QUICK TIP
Use the Restroom!

It's a good idea to use the bathroom before you enter the testing room. The certification exam is 4 hours and 15 minutes long, and there are no scheduled breaks. You may take a break if you need one, but you may not leave the testing facility, will have to go through security again, and will not be given extra time on the exam. That said, before going back to the items you flagged for review, it might be a good idea to take an unscheduled break to use the restroom, splash water on your face, stretch, or loosen up tense shoulders.

QUICK TIP
Ask for Headphones

Blocking out noise can help you concentrate during the exam. You will not be allowed to bring your own earplugs or headphones, but the test center will provide noise-blocking earphones if you need them. Just ask for noise-canceling headsets when you check in.

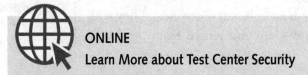

ONLINE
Learn More about Test Center Security

https://www.prometric.com/en-us/for-test-takers/pages/Test-Center-Security.aspx

Table 13.2. Acceptable Forms of Identification

Name on Application	Name on ID	Admitted to Test
Jamie Taylor-Smith	Jamie Smith	Yes
Nancy Porter	Nancy White	No
William B. Johnson	Bill Johnson	No
P. J. Miller	Peter J. Miller	Yes
Samantha R. Roberts	Samantha Rose Roberts	Yes

Primary ID	Secondary ID
Driver's License	Valid employer identification card
Passport	Valid credit card with signature
Military ID	Valid bankcard with photo

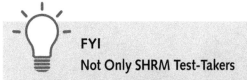

FYI
Not Only SHRM Test-Takers

Not everyone at the testing center will be taking a SHRM certification exam. In fact, the person on one side of you might be taking a CPA exam, while the person on your right might be taking a cosmetology exam. The various exams are likely to take differing amounts of time, so you can expect that people taking other exams will come and go during your exam period.

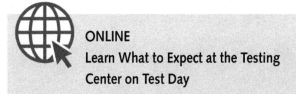

ONLINE
Learn What to Expect at the Testing Center on Test Day

https://www.prometric.com/en-us/for-test-takers
/prepare-for-test-day/Pages/overview.aspx

https://www.prometric.com/en-us/for-test-takers
/prepare-for-test-day/pages/what-to-expect.aspx

Chapter 14

Before, During, and After the Exam

Anyone who stops learning is old, whether at 20 years old or 80.

—Henry Ford

O nce you've checked in, the test center administrator will guide you to a seat at an exam computer. Make yourself comfortable and familiarize yourself with the feel of the keyboard and mouse. Use the time before the exam starts to take the exam tutorial so you'll be familiar with the computer navigation functions, especially the features for striking out obviously incorrect responses and marking or flagging questions you want to return to for review.

QUICK TIP
Preview the Exam

You can preview the exam tutorial ahead of time from your home or office computer. The tutorial explains the various features and lets you practice answering questions as well as use the features for striking out responses and flagging questions for review. You can access the tutorial at https://www .prometric.com/_layouts/SHRM/

During the exam

As you take the exam, use the strategies and tips in Parts 3 and 4 to manage your time and stay relaxed. If you need help or need to take a break, raise your hand and the TCA will come over.

Timing the exam

The total exam time is 4 hours and 15 minutes, including opening and closing activities. You will have four hours to answer the 160 multiple-choice questions on the exam itself. The countdown timer on the screen will help you keep track of the time as you progress through the questions. You can go back to any questions at any time before the 4-hour testing time is up.

Get a good night of rest prior to the exam and try to take the exam early in the day. Taking the assessment early in the day prevents hours of pre-test anxiety.

Although it's important to stay aware of the time, you don't need to feel rushed. You will have enough time to answer all the questions and take another look at those you've marked for review.

> **Breakdown of Testing Time**
>
> Candidate Confirmation Details: 2 minutes
>
> Introduction and Tutorial: 8 minutes
>
> Exam: 4 hours (240 minutes)
>
> Post-Exam Survey: 5 minutes

Pay attention to pop-up messages on the screen and don't click on "Finish" until you're done!

Pop-ups are warnings that you've hit a stray key and the computer thinks you want to finish the exam. The system asks you at least twice to confirm that you understand that if you keep clicking "Yes," you want to finish. Also, the "Finish" button in the navigation bar does not finish your review of the questions you've flagged for another look—it ends the entire exam. After you click "Finish," a pop-up window will appear asking you to confirm that you are done.

DO NOT end the exam until you are sure that you are finished. You cannot return to it once you exit. When a pop-up appears, pause, read it thoroughly, and then click the button that indicates what you want to do. DO NOT rush through the prompts, because each asks you to confirm your real intent but in a slightly different way.

If, after multiple warnings, you exit the exam, but did not mean to do so, there is no turning back. Once you confirm, you are at the point of no return and the exam will be over.

When you finish the exam

Once the exam time is up or you've hit "Finish" and confirmed that you are done, a post-test survey will pop up on the screen. The survey helps SHRM learn more about test-takers' opinions about the exam, their reasons for pursuing certification, their study and preparation methods, and their current jobs. Your responses to survey questions do not affect your test results.

> During the exam, I told myself that it was going to be a good learning experience even if I don't pass, and next time I'll know what to expect. So, it was quite a shock to see the big green check mark with the word 'Pass'!

After you finish the survey, the computer will give you a preliminary "Pass" or "Fail" notification. Prometric will also send you a copy of the preliminary results by email. Be sure to check your Spam folder if the email doesn't arrive.

When the exam is over

Congratulate yourself! Completing this rigorous test is a significant accomplishment, and you deserve a reward for all your hard work, so do something nice for yourself!

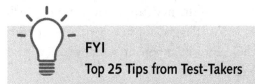

FYI

Top 25 Tips from Test-Takers

1. Make this test your biggest priority for several months prior to the test!

2. Set aside time to study and prepare your family for the time commitment proper preparation will require.

3. If you are not self-disciplined, take a prep course, in-person or virtual!

4. Understand that there is NO WAY to retain all the information covered in the materials. Memorize principles, not facts.

5. Connect with any learning group for the SHRM test preparation.

6. Know your study style.

7. Utilize the practice exams, both pre- and post- ones, to help you prepare.

8. Understand the scenarios in order to apply the best approach.

9. Understand the word to apply it (not just the definition).

10. Relax. If you've been in HR for any length of time, you likely have the knowledge, but don't realize it!

11. Keep a positive and open mind about the test and *know* you will pass if you take the time to read each question more than once, as well as the answers.

12. Download the Quizlet app on phone, iPad or another device; it helped me a lot with definitions.

13. Read the daily digest and listen to what your fellow test-takers say. Their advice was really helpful and helped me know what to expect in the exam.

14. USE the Learning System—it is a great preparation tool.

15. Take those flash cards with you so you can review them whenever you have a few moments time.

16. After studying diligently, take some time off the week of the exam for final review, then take a break from study the day before the exam.

17. Set an exam time when you are physically, and mentally sharpest, early afternoon was best for me, making sure you eat a high-protein meal before the exam.

18. Approach questions as if they were your own problems; rely on your experience, not what you think is the 'right' answer.

19. Always think about the bottom line when given options and choose the ACTION items.

20. Take an educated guess and flag the question for review and move on.

21. Remember to give yourself enough time to answer flagged questions.

22. Remain calm and confident during the exam. Go with your gut and do not change your answers.

23. Believe in yourself.

24. Relax; it's just a test, and it can be retaken.

25. Celebrate no matter what happens.

During the Exam

- Use your test-taking tips and relaxation strategies
- Keep your eye on the time
- Use the dry erase board with markers to make notes as needed
- Use the on-screen calculator (provided and permitted for use) for all calculations.
- Stay focused and think positively!
- No matter what the results, reward yourself for finishing the exam!

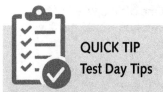

QUICK TIP
Test Day Tips

The Week Before Your Test

- Say "no" to extra commitments to give yourself plenty of time to finish your study plan.

- Check out the test location in advance: take a trial run to work out transit or driving time and parking so that you are not rushed or panicked the morning of the exam.

- Review all your notes at least once the week before your exam.

- Review all other study aids to refresh important points.

- Concentrate and apply extra study efforts to weak areas.

- Before test day or during the introductory period before the exam begins, take the exam tutorial to become familiar with the computer navigation features and practice answering the exam questions.

- Keep the day before your exam as commitment-free as possible so you can relax and review, and to organize what you need to take with you, such as your Authorization to Test (ATT) letter and your ID.

- Don't try to cram at the last minute.

- Get a good night's sleep the night before the exam.

The Day of Your Exam

- Make sure you have your photo ID and Authorization to Test letter with you when you leave for the test center.

- Plan to arrive at least 30 minutes early, and leave extra time for traffic or transit delays.

- Eat a light but healthy meal before you leave for the test center.

- Leave everything you don't need at home or in your car.

- Use the bathroom before you enter the testing room.

Appendices

Appendix 1: Practice Questions & Answers

Appendix 2: Scoring the SHRM Certification Exams

Appendix 3: Glossary of Terms Used in the Exams

Appendix 4: List of Acronyms

Appendix 5: Online Resources

Appendix 6: Selected Reading List

Appendix 1
Practice Questions & Answers

Introduction: SHRM Study Guide Practice Questions

Twenty questions previously administered on SHRM certification operational test forms are included in this appendix to allow you, as an aspiring SHRM-certification holder, the opportunity to practice taking multiple choice questions. These practice questions, like the operational exam forms, are divided into sections. First, a knowledge and foundational knowledge section appears with seven (7) items. Second, a six-item situational judgment item section appears. This section is composed of two, three-item situational judgment item sets. The final group of practice questions presents another seven-item knowledge and foundational knowledge set.

One very important caution: do not assume that ability to answer these 20 practice questions correctly equates to a passing score on the certification exam. Similarly, do not use the results of your performance on these 20 questions or on a SHRM Learning System practice test to predict how well you will do on the certification exam itself. The 20 practice questions represent less than ¼ of the number of items on an operational exam. These questions provide you the opportunity to preview the structure and format of test questions, but it is not appropriate to use results to predict an outcome on the operational exam.

Additionally, the conditions in your at-home or in-office environment will not match or likely mirror the controlled environment of a test administration center. This is why we state that these practice items are intended only to give you an idea of the way that questions are written on the operational exam, and that doing well this 20-item practice question set is not a guarantee of a passing result on the exam. Refer to chapter 7 for more information on scoring and exam construction of the operational exams.

Each SHRM-CP and SHRM-SCP operational exam is composed of 160 items, 30 of which are unscored, field-test items. The operational exam items, totaling 130 in number, are used to generate a pass/fail decision. The 160 total items are divided into five, 32-item sets and are administered in the following order:

- 32 knowledge and foundational knowledge items
- 32 situational judgment items divided into item sets
- 32 knowledge and foundational knowledge items
- 32 situational judgment items divided into item sets
- 32 knowledge and foundational knowledge items

SHRM recommends that you take practice items during a timed period to gauge your ability to complete the 20-item practice question set under timed conditions. We suggest you allot 1.5 minutes per question to gauge your ability to answer questions under time constraints.

The answer key and accompanying rationales for the correct answers for knowledge and foundational knowledge items appears at the end of the 20-item set of practice questions. For situational judgment items, the answer key represents the best response, or most effective course of action, in the situation and is determined by a panel of SHRM-certified experts. Use the following guideposts as a reminder of how situational judgment tests are written; keep this information in mind as you respond to situational judgment items on the exam.

HR professionals provide the "raw materials" for situational judgment items: critical incidents drawn from real-life situations. HR professionals also provide multiple, plausible courses of action to take in the situation, with possible actions ranging from very ineffective to very effective. Scoring panels, also composed of seasoned HR professionals, rate the various responses to identify the "best" or "most effective" response. Because the best answer is based on expert judgments, no rationale exists other than the aggregated opinion of the panelists.

If you decide to take these practice questions while timing yourself, remember to use 1.5 minutes per question, which is 30 minutes total, for the 20-item practice questions. Good luck!

Practice Questions

This section is composed of knowledge items.

1. Which method is recommended as the most effective way to provide feedback during an employee's performance evaluation?

    A. Begin with positive comments, express specific performance areas where improvement is needed, then end the discussion with additional positive remarks.
    B. Have the employee complete a self-assessment of performance, then discuss the assessment during the employee's performance evaluation.
    C. Begin by identifying the employee's performance issues and areas needing improvement, then end the discussion with positive comments.
    D. Begin with a general discussion about work activities and processes, then identify areas where improvement is needed.

2. At which phase of the strategic planning process can HR allocate resources to specific actions?

    A. Strategy formulation
    B. Strategy review
    C. Strategy development
    D. Strategy implementation

3. How can an HR manager calculate the monthly turnover in a company?

   A. [Number of total monthly separations (excluding layoffs) / average number of employees on the payroll during the month] × 100

   B. Number of unexpected separations during the month

   C. (Average number of separations per month / number of employees staying per month) × 100

   D. [Number of total monthly separations (including layoffs) / average number of employees on the payroll during the month] × 100

4. Which approach to expatriate compensation is best for an organization to use if the top priority is ensuring equity between expatriates and employees in the host country?

   A. Balance sheet

   B. Lump sum

   C. Localization

   D. Negotiation

5. Which statement best describes the primary rationale for why businesses choose to develop and implement a corporate social responsibility strategy?

   A. Meets required legal and regulatory standards

   B. Leads to positive changes in attitudes and behaviors

   C. Satisfies a moral imperative of acting as a good citizen

   D. Results in a better understanding of issues that impact society

6. A CEO approaches an HR director for help identifying future leaders of the company. What should the HR director suggest?

   A. Implement internal candidate promotion program where employees can request leadership positions.

   B. Perform surveys by department to provide input on their next leader.

    C. Request recommendations from the management team.

    D. Perform behavioral assessments to determine employees' personal characteristics and qualities.

7. Which consideration is most important when designing incentive programs with rewards based on improvements in work group productivity?

    A. Level of cooperativeness in the workplace

    B. Proportion of an employee's salary that is linked to variable pay

    C. Value of the incentive relative to an employee's stock options

    D. Extent to which the incentive program significantly affects profits

This section is composed of situational judgment items.

The following scenario accompanies the next three (3) items.

A large consumer goods company with geographically dispersed employees and a bureaucratic organizational structure seeks to create a participative and inclusive culture by requiring employees to communicate and collaborate across product lines. The company changes its existing structure by shifting work between locations, reducing the size of its management team, and eliminating a major product line. Despite these changes, employees find it difficult to develop strong relationship ties given the lack of organizational support, schedule conflicts, and strict policies.

    The company's HR manager hires an early career HR professional to explore changing the organizational culture and improving communication among employees, customers, and stakeholders across different geographic locations. The HR professional proposes an employee recognition program that encourages collaborative behavior by awarding an outstanding employee with an opportunity to give a presentation to the CEO on the importance of workplace collaboration. The HR manager rejects the proposal due to concerns about the effectiveness of a presentation for fostering an inclusive work environment. Confident that recognizing collaborative behavior is the best approach to participation and inclusion, the HR professional proposes a recognition program that gives employees an opportunity to select the most collaborative employees through an HR technology system. The HR professional's approach to the employee recognition program is a unique idea but needs design and delivery assistance.

The HR professional receives positive feedback from other early career professionals working outside of HR on the various ideas and suggestions for new approaches.

8. Which design solution is best for the HR professional to recommend to change the culture across the entire company?

   A. Include feedback from focus groups to ensure that all stakeholder voices are heard and acknowledged.

   B. Link the program to the company's vision of employee collaboration across product lines and geographic locations.

   C. Recognize geographically-dispersed employees who collaborate despite schedule conflicts and high travel costs.

   D. Review program details and meet with the HR manager to ensure understanding of expectations.

9. Which action is best for the HR professional to take first after concluding that the HR technology systems currently available in the company do not support the project?

   A. Prepare a cost-benefit analysis of the survey technology platforms with the required features and request funding to support the purchase.

   B. Determine if the desired technology exists in other internal business units and assess the HR department's willingness to participate.

   C. Develop a manual solution that accomplishes the same objective and ensure the availability of an employee network to complete the work.

   D. Adapt the current HR technology design so that it supports the project and modify if needed as the program continues to grow.

10. Which action should the HR professional take to increase the level of interest in the program among employees who provide positive feedback and suggestions for new approaches?

   A. Refer them to a page on the company's intranet containing more information about the new program.
   B. Ask them to forward related project ideas that they are interested in working on later in the project.
   C. Include them in an email group and send more information as the project progresses.
   D. Share program information with them and ask them to quickly distribute that information to their coworkers.

The following scenario accompanies the next three (3) items.

A technology start-up company has recently hired 100 new employees over the span of a month. Due to so many people being hired in such a short period of time, the small HR department has struggled to consistently onboard all new employees. Some HR staff have thoroughly explained company policies and procedures to new employees, while others have not. Managers are submitting complaints that many of the new employees lack basic knowledge about company policies and procedures, resulting in lost productivity. The HR manager, who has been with the company for three months, has been asked to help solve this problem.

11. Which action should the HR manager take to ensure that all new employees going forward receive onboarding when they join the organization?

   A. Communicate to all managers that it is now their responsibility to onboard new employees.
   B. Review onboarding procedures with HR staff to create a checklist for onboarding new employees.
   C. Develop a central website to refer all new employees for onboarding information.
   D. Review the current onboarding program to make necessary improvements.

12. Several of the new employees have told the HR manager that they made some mistakes due to the lack of knowledge of procedures, and they are concerned their managers no longer trust them. What should the HR manager do to address their concerns?

    A. Hold a meeting with their managers to explain the onboarding issues with new employees and how HR is correcting the problem.
    B. Send out a company-wide email explaining that some new employees may not be familiar with company policies and procedures due to the onboarding issue.
    C. Tell the new employees that it takes time to build trust with their managers.
    D. Conduct a team building training for the employees and their managers related to trust building.

13. The HR manager decides to make a more standardized orientation process for new employees. Which is the most effective method of developing the content for the orientation?

    A. Ask other HR employees in a professional network about the content included in their orientation processes.
    B. Conduct a training needs analysis of new employees and include content on areas in which they consistently lack knowledge.
    C. Ask managers in the company what information they need new employees to learn from an orientation process.
    D. Hire an agency to conduct, review and design a new orientation process.

This section is composed of knowledge items.

14. Which objective is consistent with Locke's theory when establishing goals?

    A. Answer customer queries as quickly as possible.
    B. Investigate absence levels and recommend solutions.

C. Recruit 50 new customers before the end of the year.

D. Carry out quarterly analyses and improve customer satisfaction.

15. Which is considered a method used to provide on-the-job management development?

A. Coaching

B. Simulation

C. Role play

D. Conference

16. Which type of social media should an HR manager use to most effectively provide identified candidates with continuous updates about current organizational events and activities?

A. Microblogging

B. Professional networks

C. Podcasting

D. Content-driven communities

17. Which action most accurately reflects an HR manager's responsibility for supporting workforce planning?

A. Creating qualified candidate pools

B. Interviewing candidates for open positions

C. Selecting candidates with the best organizational fit

D. Highlighting the performance potential of best candidates

18. A company has decided to transfer key project engineers to an overseas project site. Which step should HR take first to ensure a fair compensation system for all employees regardless of their location?

A. Design a new compensation package including merit pay for the transferred employees.

B. Convert the engineers' salaries to the host country's currency.

C. Provide relocation assistance to transferred employees.

    D. Implement cost-of-living adjustments for all trans-
       ferred employees.

19. Which OSHA elements must an HR manager include when
creating an emergency action plan?

    A. An alternative communications center
    B. List of beneficiaries and primary care providers of all
       employees
    C. Description of the system used to notify employees of the
       need to evacuate
    D. Procedures to account for all employees after an evacuation

20. Which aspect of diversity and inclusion training is the most
effective for resolving conflict?

    A. Negating stereotypes about group members from different
       backgrounds
    B. Highlighting similarities of employees from different
       backgrounds
    C. Encouraging employees from minority backgrounds to
       assimilate with the cultural majority
    D. Encouraging tolerance of employees from different
       backgrounds

End of Practice Questions

Answer Keys

Knowledge items have a correct response and the situational judgment
items have a best or most effective response; both are known as the *Key*.

- For knowledge and foundational knowledge items, there is one
correct answer and three incorrect answers. Rationales explain why
the correct answer for each knowledge or foundational item is
correct.

- *Unlike knowledge-based items,* situational judgment items have no one "correct" answer, only degrees of effectiveness, based on the judgment of a group of subject matter experts. While more than one of the possible strategies might be effective, one will be best, given the situation and as decided by a panel of SHRM-certified HR professionals.

The answer keys with rationales for the 20 practice questions follow:

Question Number	Key	Rationale
Knowledge Items		
1	A	Start and end with positive feedback, but include the negative feedback, developmental information, and reinforce performance expectations in the middle of the discussion is the best course of action. The other options focus on components of a performance management process that occur at other points in the process, but not during the performance discussion or would not be the first or only discussion topics during the performance discussion.
2	D	Strategy implementation is the phase during which resources are allocated to various actions included in the strategy. Resource allocation does not occur at the formulation, review or development phase of a strategy.
3	A	Monthly turnover is accurately calculated only by the formula shown in the first option. The other three calculations are either missing a factor or include a factor not used to calculate monthly turnover.
4	C	Localization is the best compensation approach to use when striving to achieve pay equity between expatriates sent on international assignment and host-country nationals already working in the country.
5	C	Corporate social responsibility (CSR) programs are primarily implemented so the organization can do good works as part of programs that benefit the local community and serve as a way of giving back to that community. While CSR programs may lead to improved attitudes and a better understanding of the community, neither is a primary reason for implementing a CSR program. CSR programs are generally not regulated programs; thus, implementing one to meet legal requirements is not a primary reason to do so.

Question Number	Key	Rationale
6	D	Perform behavioral assessments to reveal employee's personal characteristics and qualities is the correct answer. Forward thinking companies value this scientific tool because the quantitative and qualitative information revealed in a behavioral assessment can be measured with the qualifications of a job. The other answers are based on opinions and volunteering for the job.
7	A	Cooperation among team members is the most important design consideration if the organization wishes to incent group productivity. Stock options and profit margins are not a consideration if incenting team productivity is the goal; percentage of pay linked to the incentive is not the most important design consideration.
Situational Judgment Item Sets		*Note*: Unlike knowledge items, situational judgment items do not have a rationale. See explanation below about how the best or most effective course of action is derived by expert panelists.
8	B	Situational judgment tests (SJTs) require the examinee to think about what is occurring in the scenario and decide which response option identifies the most effective course of action. Other response options may be something you *could* do to respond in the situation, but SJTs require thinking and acting based on the best of the available options. Do not base your answer on your organization's approach to handling the situation, but rather, answer based on what you know *should* be done according to best practice. Panels of SHRM-certified subject matter experts rate the effectiveness of each response option, and the "best" answer is derived by statistical analysis of those expert opinions.
9	B	
10	C	
11	B	
12	A	
13	B	
Knowledge Items		
14	C	Recruit 50 new customers before the end of year has the specific and measurable components that are hallmarks of Locke's theory. The other three options are vague and do not include specific benchmarks to measure goal achievement.
15	A	Coaching is the approach that specifically addresses on-the-job management behavior improvement. Role play, simulation and conference may be tools used during coaching, but coaching provides the overall framework to address improvement of behavior for management team members.

Question Number	Key	Rationale
16	A	Microblogging provides an efficient and expeditious way for recruiters to communicate updated information to candidates who have been identified to proceed to the next stage in the recruitment process.
17	A	To support the organization's overall workforce development plans, the HR manager's most important responsibility is to develop and create a diverse pool of qualified candidates. While interviewing and selecting candidates and subsequently highlighting components of high-performing individuals are important for implementing a workforce development plan, the critical first step is to attract qualified candidates to meet the organization's workforce needs.
18	D	Cost-of-living adjustments give the same percent increase across-the-board to everyone, regardless of performance, and based on the actual cost of living where the organization is located. Other options may be appropriate, but only after determining whether a change in base salary is needed based on the cost to live in the organization's specific location.
19	D	OSHA provides guidance on establishing a wide variety of steps to take in response to an emergency, including establishing an alternative communication center, providing lists of medical service providers and writing an effective announcement to motivate employees to evacuate. However, regarding the most important thing for an HR manager to include in the plan itself, that is to establish and communicate the protocol staff must use to account for every employee post-evacuation. After everyone is accounted for, other components of the plan can be implemented.
20	B	In diversity and inclusion training, focusing on commonalities is best; highlighting commonalities among employees of different backgrounds—rather than focusing on differences, requiring employees to adjust or attempting to negate stereotypes—will best help the organization resolve conflict.

Appendix 2

Scoring the SHRM Certification Exams

Some people have asked us how the SHRM-CP and SHRM-SCP certification examinations are scored, and how those scores are reported to examinees. The most frequently asked questions include:

- Why is 200 the passing score when the exam has 160 questions?
- Do I have to earn the maximum score to pass the exam?
- What is the number of questions I must answer correctly to pass the exam?
- What is the number of questions I must answer correctly in the SHRM Learning System to know whether I will pass the exam?

First, we would like to describe how we set the passing scores for the SHRM certification exams. We employ best-practice procedures most commonly used for setting performance standards for certification and licensure exams. During a multiday evaluation process, a panel of experienced HR professionals evaluates the exam questions to determine how difficult they are for a candidate who is "just qualified" at the appropriate level—SHRM-CP (for early- to mid-career HR professionals) or SHRM-SCP (for senior-level HR professionals).

To keep the SHRM certification exams up-to-date and fair, we add and remove questions during every testing window. Before a new question is used, it is first pretested with real examinees. We do that by mixing 30 pretest questions (" field test items") into each exam. Test-takers answer the pretest questions, but answers to pretest questions are not part of the pass decision. In other words, of the 160 questions on the exam that you answer, 130 are used to calculate your score; the 30 pretest items do not count. Because there is no way for you to know which questions count toward your score and which do not, it is important to do your best on *all* test items.

After the field-test items are pretested, SHRM analyzes their performance. Only those questions that meet the performance standards become scored items on subsequent exams.

Raw scores and scaled scores

After you take the test, you will have a *raw score* of 0-130 correct answers; but the score we report to you is *on a scale* of 120-200, with "passing" set at 200—this is known as your *scaled score*.

It is a common and best practice in standardized testing to place the number of questions answered correctly on a scale (scaled score), rather than to simply report the number of questions answered correctly (raw score). You may be familiar with this process if you have taken the SAT or ACT for college, the GRE for a master's degree, or the GMAT for a master's degree in business administration. The scores for these exams range from 400–1600 for the SAT, 1–36 for the ACT, 130–170 for the GRE, and 200–800 for the GMAT. Just like on the SHRM-CP and SHRM-SCP exams, the numbers of questions on these tests differ from their reported scores.

What is the "200" all about?

For the SHRM exams, 200 is not necessarily a perfect score. We do not report scores above 200 because anyone who passes the SHRM-CP or SHRM-SCP exam is considered to have achieved the competency level required to earn certification. We could just report a pass/fail result; instead, we provide all candidates with a score report that shows on a graph how well they did in the different competency and knowledge sub-areas. This additional information can help test-takers evaluate their strengths and weaknesses. Unsuccessful candidates have a numerical score that shows them how close they were to being successful, plus a non-numerical score report to help them make appropriate choices about preparing for future exams. For successful candidates, the score report serves as feedback on their performance that can help guide their recertification plans and professional development activities.

The SHRM-CP and SHRM-SCP exams—like the SAT, ACT, GRE and GMAT—have been developed using rigorous methodologies and procedures. The exams include a combination of low-, medium- and high-difficulty questions. While we try to make sure the distribution of difficulty is the same on every exam, it is practically impossible to guarantee that each exam is equally difficult. Therefore, we use a statistical process called *equating* to match the raw scores from a particular test with the scaled scores from that test. This is to ensure that test-takers are not unfairly penalized or rewarded for having taken an exam that was more or less difficult than another exam given at another time for the same certification.

Equating is one reason why we cannot reveal the number of questions you need to answer correctly to get a passing score. The number of correct questions you need to pass *your* exam may differ slightly from the number of correct questions another candidate needs to pass a different exam.

We do not compare SHRM certification test-takers against one other—that is, the exams are *not* scored on what is commonly known as a curve. (In technical terms, the exams are not "normed.") If everyone who takes their test meets the knowledge and competency standards, everyone will pass. The opposite is also true. If no one who takes the test meets the knowledge and competency standards, no one will pass.

Appendix 3

Glossary of Terms Used in the Exams

The following terms appear in the SHRM Body of Competency and Knowledge (BoCK), may appear on the SHRM-CP and SHRM-SCP certification exams, and are applicable to all examinees.

ADDIE (analysis, design, development, implementation, and evaluation) model: Instructional systems design (ISD) framework consisting of five steps that guide the design and development of learning programs.

Alternative dispute resolution (ADR): Umbrella term for the various approaches and techniques, other than litigation, that can be used to resolve a dispute (e.g., arbitration, conciliation, mediation).

Analytics: Tools that add context or sub-classifying comparison groups to data so that the data can be used for decision support.

Applicant: Person who has applied for or formally expressed interest in a position.

Applicant tracking system (ATS): Software application that automates organizations' management of the recruiting process (e.g., accepting application materials, screening applicants).

Arbitration: Method of alternative dispute resolution (ADR) by which disputing parties agree to be bound by the decision of one or more impartial persons to whom they submit their dispute for final determination.

Assessment center: Process by which job candidates or employees are evaluated to determine their suitability and/or readiness for employment, training, promotion or an assignment.

Balance sheet: Statement of an organization's financial position at a specific point in time, showing assets, liabilities and shareholder equity.

Balanced scorecard: Performance management tool that depicts an organization's overall performance, as measured against goals, lagging indicators and leading indicators.

Benchmarking: Process by which an organization identifies performance gaps and sets goals for performance improvement, by comparing its data, performance levels and/or processes against those of other organizations.

Benefits: Mandatory or voluntary payments or services provided to employees, typically covering retirement, health care, sick pay/disability, life insurance and paid time off (PTO).

Bias: Conscious or unconscious beliefs that influence a person's perceptions or actions, which may cause that person to become partial or prejudiced.

Bona fide occupational qualification (BFOQ): Factor (e.g., gender, religion, national origin) that is reasonably necessary, in the normal operations of an organization, to carry out a particular job function.

Business case: Tool or document that defines a specific problem, proposes a solution, and provides justifications for the proposal in terms of time, cost efficiency and probability of success.

Business intelligence: Raw data, internal and external to an organization, that is translated into meaningful information for decision makers to use in taking strategic action.

Business unit: Element or segment of an organization that represents a specific business function (e.g., accounting, marketing, production); also, may be called department, division, group, cost center or functional area.

Buy-in: Process by which a person or group provides a sustained commitment in support of a decision, approach, solution or course of action.

Career development: Progression through a series of employment stages characterized by relatively unique issues, themes and tasks.

Career mapping: Process by which organizations use visual tools or guides to depict prototypical or exemplary career possibilities and paths, in terms of sequential positions, roles and stages.

Career pathing: Process by which employers provide employees with a clear outline for moving from a current to a desired position.

Cash flow statement: Statement of an organization's ability to meet its current and short-term obligations, showing incoming and outgoing cash and cash reserves in operations, investments and financing.

Center of excellence (COE): Team or structure that provides expertise, best practices, support and/or knowledge transfer in a focused area.

Change initiative: Transition in an organization's technology, culture or behavior of its employees and managers.

Change management: Principles and practices for managing a change initiative so that it is more likely to be accepted and provided with the resources (financial, human, physical, etc.) necessary to reshape the organization and its people.

Coaching: Focused, interactive communication and guidance intended to develop and enhance on-the-job performance, knowledge or behavior.

Collective bargaining: Process by which management and union representatives negotiate the employment conditions for a particular bargaining unit for a designated period of time.

Comparable worth: Concept that jobs primarily filled by women, which require skills, effort, responsibility and working conditions comparable to similar jobs primarily filled by men, should have the same classifications and salaries.

Competencies: Clusters of highly interrelated attributes, including knowledge, skills, abilities and other characteristics (KSAOs), that give rise to the behaviors needed to perform a given job effectively.

Compliance: State of being in accordance with all national, federal, regional and/or local laws, regulations and/or other government authorities and requirements applicable to the places in which an organization operates.

Conciliation: Method of nonbinding alternative dispute resolution (ADR) by which a neutral third party tries to help disputing parties reach a mutually agreeable decision (i.e., mediation).

Conflict of interest: Situation in which a person or organization may potentially benefit, directly or indirectly, from undue influence, due to involvement in outside activities, relationships or investments that conflict with or have an impact on the employment relationship or its outcomes.

Corporate social responsibility (CSR): Concept that a corporation has an impact on the lives of its stakeholders and the environment, encompassing such areas as corporate governance, philanthropy, sustainability, employee rights, social change, volunteerism, corporate-sponsored community programs and workplace safety.

Cost-benefit analysis (CBA): Approach to determining the financial impact of an organization's activities and programs on profitability, through a process of data or calculation comparing value created against the cost of creating that value.

Critical path: Amount of time needed to complete all required elements or components of a task, determined by taking into account all project-task relationships.

Culture: Basic beliefs, attitudes, values, behaviors and customs shared and followed by members of a group, which give rise to the group's sense of identity.

Disability: Physical or mental impairment that substantially limits one's major life activities.

Diversity: Differences in people's characteristics (e.g., age, beliefs, education, ethnicity, gender, job function, personality, race, religion, socioeconomic status, thought processes, work style).

Due diligence: Requirement to thoroughly investigate an action before it is taken, through diligent research and evaluation.

E-learning: Electronic media delivery of educational and training materials, processes and programs.

Emotional intelligence (EI): Ability to be sensitive to and understand one's own and others' emotions and impulses.

Employee engagement: Employees' emotional commitment to an organization, demonstrated by their willingness to put in discretionary effort to promote the organization's effective functioning.

Employee surveys: Instruments that collect and assess information on employees' attitudes and perceptions (e.g., engagement, job satisfaction) of the work environment or employment conditions.

Employee value proposition (EVP): Employees' perceived value of the total rewards and tangible and intangible benefits they receive from the organization as part of employment, which drives unique and compelling organizational strategies for talent acquisition, retention and engagement.

Employees: Persons who exchange their work for wages or salary.

Ethics: Set of behavioral guidelines that an organization expects all of its directors, managers and employees to follow, in order to ensure appropriate moral and ethical business standards.

Evidence-based: Approach to evaluation and decision-making that utilizes data and research findings to drive business outcomes.

Focus group: Small group of invited persons (typically six to twelve) who actively participate in a structured discussion, led by a facilitator, for the purpose of eliciting their input on a specific product, process, policy or program.

Gap analysis: Method of assessing a current state in order to determine what is needed to move to a desired future state.

Global mindset: Ability to have an international perspective, inclusive of other cultures' views.

Globalization: Status of growing interconnectedness and interdependency among countries, people, markets and organizations worldwide.

Governance: System of rules and processes set up by an organization to ensure its compliance with local and international laws, accounting rules, ethical norms, internal codes of conduct and other standards.

Hazard: Potential harm, often associated with a condition or activity that, if left uncontrolled, can result in injury or damage to persons or property.

HR business partner: HR professional who advises an organization's leaders in developing and implementing a human capital strategy that closely aligns with overall organizational mission, vision and goals.

HR service model: Approach to structuring and delivering an organization's HR services to support organizational success.

Human resource information system (HRIS): Information technology (IT) framework and tools for gathering, storing, maintaining, retrieving, revising and reporting relevant HR data.

Inclusion: Extent to which each person in an organization feels welcomed, respected, supported and valued as a team member.

Individual development plan (IDP): Document that guides employees toward their goals for professional development and growth.

Information management (IM): Use of technology to collect, process and condense information to manage the information efficiently as an organizational resource.

Integrity: Adherence to a set of ethical standards, reflecting strong moral principles, honesty and consistency in behavior.

Internal equity: Extent to which employees perceive that monetary and other rewards are distributed equitably, based on effort, skill and/or relevant outcomes.

Job analysis: Process of systematically studying a job to identify the activities/tasks and responsibilities it includes, the personal qualifications necessary to perform it, and the conditions under which it is performed.

Job description: Document that describes a job and its essential functions and requirements (e.g., knowledge, skills, abilities, tasks, reporting structure, responsibilities).

Job enlargement: Process of broadening a job's scope by adding different tasks to the job.

Job enrichment: Process of increasing a job's depth by adding responsibilities to the job.

Job evaluation: Process of determining a job's value and price to attract and retain employees, by comparing the job against other jobs within the organization or against similar jobs in competing organizations.

Key performance indicators (KPIs): Quantifiable measures of performance that gauge an organization's progress toward strategic objectives or other agreed-upon performance standards.

KSAOs: Knowledge, skills, abilities and other characteristics.

Labor union: Group of workers who formally organize and coordinate their activities to achieve common goals in their relationship with an employer or group of employers (i.e., trade union).

Lagging indicator: Type of metric describing an activity or change in performance that has already occurred.

Leader development: Professional program that helps management- and executive-level employees develop knowledge, skills, abilities and other characteristics (KSAOs) related to leadership.

Leadership: Ability to influence, guide, inspire or motivate a group or person to achieve their goals.

Leading indicator: Type of metric describing an activity that can change future performance and predict success in the achievement of strategic goals.

Liabilities: Organization's debts and other financial obligations.

Measurement: Process of collecting, quantifying and evaluating data.

Mediation: Method of nonbinding alternative dispute resolution (ADR) by which a neutral third party tries to help disputing parties reach a mutually agreeable decision (i.e., conciliation).

Mentoring: Relationship in which one person helps guide another's development.

Merger & acquisition (M&A): Process by which two separate organizations combine, either by joining together as relative equals (merger) or by one procuring the other (acquisition).

Mission statement: Concise outline of an organization's strategy, specifying the activities it intends to pursue and the course its management has charted for the future.

Motivation: Factors that initiate, direct and sustain human behavior over time.

Negotiation: Process by which two or more parties work together to reach agreement on a matter.

Offshoring: Method by which an organization relocates its processes or production to an international location through subsidiaries or third-party affiliates.

Onboarding: Process of assimilating new employees into an organization through orientation programs to help them. New employees' experiences in their first months of employment.

Organizational effectiveness: Degree to which an organization is successful in executing its strategic objectives and mission.

Organizational learning: Acquisition and/or transfer of knowledge within an organization through activities or processes that may occur at several organizational levels. Ability of an organization to learn from its mistakes and adjust its strategy accordingly.

Organizational values: Beliefs and principles defined by an organization to direct and govern its employees' behavior.

Orientation: Process by which new employees become familiar with the organization and with their specific department, coworkers and job.

Outsourcing: Process by which an organization contracts with third-party vendors to provide selected services/activities, instead of hiring new employees.

Performance appraisal: Process of measuring and evaluating an employee's adherence to performance standards and providing feedback to the employee.

Performance management: Tools, activities and processes that an organization uses to manage, maintain and/or improve the job performance of employees.

Performance measures: Data or calculations comparing current performance against key performance indicators (KPIs).

Performance standards: Behaviors and results defined by an organization to communicate the expectations of management.

Pluralism: Type of labor environment in which multiple forces are at work in an organization, each with its own agenda, and in which conflict is overcome through negotiation.

Position: Scope of work roles and responsibilities associated with one or more persons.

Radicalism: Concept that management-labor conflict is an inherent characteristic of capitalism and can be resolved only with a change in the economic system.

Realistic job preview (RJP): Tool used in the staffing/selection process to provide an applicant with honest, complete information about the job and work environment.

Recruitment: Process by which an organization seeks out candidates and encourages them to apply for job openings.

Regulation: Rule or order issued by an administrative agency of government, which usually has the force of law.

Reliability: Extent to which a measurement instrument provides consistent results.

Remediation: Process by which an unacceptable action or behavior is corrected.

Remuneration: Total pay in the form of salary and wages received in exchange for employment (e.g., allowances, benefits, bonuses, cash incentives, monetary value of non-cash incentives).

Remuneration surveys: Instruments that collect information on prevailing market compensation and benefits practices (e.g., base pay, pay ranges, starting wage rates, statutory and market cash payments, paid time off [PTO], variable compensation).

Repatriation: Process by which employees returning from international assignments reintegrate into their home country's culture, conditions and employment.

Restructuring: Act of reorganizing the legal, ownership, operational or other structures of an organization.

Retention: Ability of an organization to keep its employees.

Return on investment (ROI): Data or calculation comparing an investment's monetary or intrinsic value against expended resources.

Risk: Uncertainty with an effect on an objective, where effect outcomes may include opportunities, losses and threats.

Risk management: System for identifying, evaluating and controlling actual and potential risks to an organization, and which typically incorporate mitigation and/or response strategies, including the use of insurance.

Selection: Process of evaluating the most suitable candidates for a position.

Six Sigma/Lean Six Sigma: A set of techniques and tools for process improvement, aimed at increasing quality by decreasing defects in processes. Lean Six Sigma also aims at increasing speed by eliminating waste.

Social media: Internet technology platforms and communities that people and organizations use to communicate and share information, opinions and resources.

Socialization: Process by which persons learn the knowledge, language, social skills, culture and values required for assimilating into a group or organization.

Sourcing: Process by which an organization generates a pool of qualified job applicants.

Stakeholders: Those affected by an organization's social, environmental and economic impact (e.g., customers, employees, local communities, regulators, shareholders, suppliers).

Stay interviews: Structured conversations with employees for the purpose of determining which aspects of a job (e.g., culture, engagement, leadership, organization, satisfaction) encourage employee retention, or may be improved to do so.

Strategic management: System of actions that leaders take to drive an organization toward its goals and objectives.

Strategic planning: Process of setting goals and designing a path toward organizational success.

Strategy: Plan of action for accomplishing an organization's overall and long-range goals.

Succession planning: Process of implementing a talent management strategy to identify and foster the development of high-potential employees or other job candidates who, over time, may move into leadership positions of increased responsibility.

Sustainability: Practice of purchasing and using resources wisely by balancing economic, social and environmental concerns, toward the goal of securing present and future generations' interests.

SWOT (strength, weakness, opportunity and threat) analysis: Method for assessing an organization's strategic capabilities through the environmental scanning process, which identifies and considers the internal and external factors that affect the achievement of organizational goals and objectives.

Systems thinking: Process for understanding how seemingly independent units within a larger entity interact with and influence one another.

Talent management: System of integrated HR processes for attracting, developing, engaging and retaining employees who have the knowledge, skills, abilities and other characteristics (KSAOs) to meet current and future business needs.

Totalization agreements: Bilateral agreements between countries, entered into for the purpose of eliminating double taxation of employees on international assignments.

Trade union: Group of workers who formally organize and coordinate their activities to achieve common goals in their relationship with an employer or group of employers (i.e., labor union).

Training: Process by which employees are provided with the knowledge, skills, abilities and other characteristics (KSOAs) specific to a task or job.

Transformational leadership: Leadership style that focuses on challenging and developing members of an organization to attain long-range results through continuous evolution, improvement or change, based on the leader's vision and strategy.

Transparency: Extent to which an organization's agreements, dealings, information, practices and transactions are open to disclosure and review by relevant persons.

Turnover: Act of replacing employees who are leaving an organization. Attrition or loss of employees.

Unfair labor practice (ULP): Violation of employee rights. Action prohibited under labor-relations statutes.

Unitarism: Concept that employers and employees can act together for their common good.

Validity: Extent to which a measurement instrument measures what it is intended to measure.

Value: Measure of usefulness, worth or importance.

Variance analysis: Statistical method for identifying the degree of difference between planned and actual performance or outcomes.

Vision: Description of what an organization hopes to attain and accomplish in the future, which guides it toward that defined direction.

Workforce planning: Strategic process by which an organization analyzes its current workforce and determines the steps required for it to prepare for future needs.

Workplace accommodation: Modification of a job, job site, or way of doing a job, so that persons with disabilities can have equal access to opportunity in all aspects of work and can perform the essential functions of their positions.

Works councils: Groups that represent employees, generally on a local or organizational level, for the primary purpose of receiving from employers and conveying to employees information about the workforce and the health of the enterprise.

List of Acronyms

The following acronyms appear in the SHRM Body of Competency and Knowledge (BoCK), may appear on the SHRM-CP and SHRM-SCP certification exams, and are applicable to all examinees. There are three categories of acronyms—terms that are never spelled out and always appear as an acronym in a test item, are standard across HR practice, and are commonly understood by HR practitioners; common acronyms used in HR practice that are spelled out the first time they appear in a test item and then used as an acronym in the item thereafter; and terms that are likely to be familiar only to some HR professionals and therefore are always spelled out.

Category 1: Acronyms that are never spelled out

CEO, CFO, HR, HRIS, HRM, ISO, IT and VP.

Category 2: Common terms

On the exam, each of these terms is spelled out the first time it is used in an exam item. Its acronym will be shown in parentheses if the term is used again in that item; if the term is used only once in that item, no acronym will be shown.

ADDIE	Analysis, Design, Development, Implementation, Evaluation
ADR	Alternative Dispute Resolution
ATS	Applicant Tracking System

CHRO	Chief Human Resource Officer
COO	Chief Operating Officer
CSR	Corporate Social Responsibility
EAP	Employee Assistance Program
EVP	Employer Value Proposition
HRBP	HR Business Partner
ILO	International Labor Organization
KPI	Key Performance Indicator
KSAO	Knowledge, Skills, Abilities and Other Characteristics
M&A	Merger and Acquisition
MNC	Multinational Corporation
PESTLE	Political, Economic, Social, Technological, Legal and Environmental
PTO	Paid Time Off
ROI	Return on Investment
SWOT	Strengths, Weaknesses, Opportunities, Threats

Notes:

- For situational judgment items, the term will be spelled out and the acronym placed in parentheses the first time it is used in the scenario associated with that item. Then it will appear only as an acronym in the rest of the scenario and in each of the associated questions and possible responses.
- When a term appears more than once in a knowledge item, it will be spelled out the first time it is used in the question. Then it will appear only as an acronym in the rest of the question and possible responses.

Category 3

If SHRM has not included a term you or your organization typically use as an acronym on one of these preceding two lists, the term will be spelled out whenever it is used on the exam. This includes, **but is not**

limited to, *cost-benefit analysis, center of excellence, emotional intelligence, individual development plan, information management, learning management system, realistic job preview, research and development.*

Additional U.S. Employment Law Acronyms for U.S.-Based Examinees

The following acronyms are U.S.-specific laws, regulations or terminology that should be familiar to all U.S.-based examinees. These terms will appear only as acronyms on the exam and will not be spelled out anywhere in the exam(s). International examinees need not be familiar with these terms.

ADA	Americans with Disabilities Act
ADAAA	Americans with Disabilities Amendment Act
ADEA	Age Discrimination in Employment Act
BFOQ	Bona Fide Occupational Qualification
COBRA	Consolidated Omnibus Budget Reconciliation Act
EEOC	Equal Employment Opportunity Commission
EPA	Equal Pay Act
ERISA	Employee Retirement Income Security Act
FCRA	Fair Credit Reporting Act
FMLA	Family and Medical Leave Act
FLSA	Fair Labor Standards Act
GINA	Genetic Information Nondiscrimination Act
HIPAA	Health Insurance Portability and Accountability Act
LMRA	Labor Management Relations Act
NLRA/B	National Labor Relations Act/Board
OSHA	Occupational Safety and Health Act *(Law)* or Administration *(Agency)*
ULP	Unfair Labor Practice
WARN	Worker Adjustment and Retraining Notification Act

Online Resources

SHRM Body of Competency and Knowledge (BoCK):
https://www.shrm.org/certification/about/body-of-competency
-and-knowledge/Pages/default.aspx

Eligibility requirements for the SHRM-CP and SHRM-SCP exams:
https://www.shrm.org/certification/apply/EligibilityCriteria
/Pages/default.aspx

Application for the SHRM-CP and SHRM-SCP exams:
https://www.shrm.org/certification/apply/Pages
/applicationprocess.aspx

Recertification:
https://www.shrm.org/certification/recertification
/RecertificationRequirements/Pages/default.aspx

Prometric Testing Centers: http://www.prometric.com/SHRM

Honey and Mumford learning styles:
https://www2.le.ac.uk/departments/doctoralcollege/training
/eresources/teaching/theories/honey-mumford

SHRM Learning System:
https://www.shrm.org/certification/prepare/Pages/default.aspx

VAK/VARK model:
https://www.ccconline.org/vakvark-model/

Mind Mapping:
https://www.sheffield.ac.uk/ssid/301/study-skills/everyday-skills/mind-mapping

Active Recall:
https://www.speaktoyourmind.com/blog/active-recall

The Leitner System:
https://www.virtualsalt.com/learn10.html

The Feynman Technique:
https://evernote.com/blog/learning-from-the-feynman-technique/

Chunking:
https://www.verywellmind.com/chunking-how-can-this-technique-improve-your-memory-2794969

Local SHRM chapters:
https://www.shrm.org/search/pages/LocalChapter.aspx

Sample SHRM-CP questions:
https://lp.shrm.org/SHRMCertificationPracticeQuestions.html

SHRM Community:
https://community.shrm.org/home

Test Anxiety:
https://www.ted.com/talks/sian_leah_beilock_why_we_choke_under_pressure_and_how_to_avoid_it

https://www.einstein.yu.edu/education/student-affairs/academic-support-counseling/medical-school-challenges/test-anxiety.aspx

Procrastination:

https://www.washingtonpost.com/news/wonk/wp/2016/04/27
/why-you-cant-help-read-this-article-about-procrastination
-instead-of-doing-your-job/

https://hbr.org/2017/10/5-research-based-strategies-for
-overcoming-procrastination

Test Center Security:

https://www.prometric.com/en-us/for-test-takers/pages/Test
-Center-Security.aspx

Test day preparation:

https://www.prometric.com/en-us/for-test-takers/prepare-for
-test-day/Pages/overview.aspx

Exam tutorial:

https://www.prometric.com/_layouts/SHRM/

Appendix 6
Select Reading List

B elow is a selection of books and articles that you might find useful as you prepare for the certification exam. You'll find an expanded list at http://shrmcertification.org/SHRMBOCK /Resources.

General Resources

Dess, G. G., McNamara, G., & Eisner, A. B. *Strategic Management: Creating Competitive Advantages* (8th ed.). New York, NY: McGraw-Hill, 2016.

Dessler, G., *Fundamentals of Human Resources Management* (4th ed.) Upper Saddle River, NJ: Prentice Hall, 2015.

Gomez-Mejia, L. R., Balkin, D. B., & Cardy, R. L., *Managing Human Resources* (8th ed.). Upper Saddle River, NJ: Prentice-Hall, 2015.

McShane, S. L., & VonGlinow, M., *Organizational Behavior* (7th ed.), New York, NY: McGraw-Hill, 2014.

Leadership & Navigation

Grenny, J., Patterson, K., Maxfield, D., McMillan, R., & Switzler, A., *Influencer: The New Science of Leading Change* (2nd ed.). New York, NY: McGraw-Hill, 2013.

Scandura, T. A., *Essentials of Organizational Behavior: An Evidence-Based Approach.* Thousand Oaks, CA: SAGE Publications, Inc., 2016.

Ethical Practice

Ferrell, O. C., & Fraedrich, J., *Business Ethics: Ethical Decision Making & Cases* (11th ed.). Nelson Education, 2016.

Hartman, L. P., DesJardins, J. R., & MacDonald, C., *Business Ethics: Decision Making for Personal Integrity and Social Responsibility* (3rd ed.). New York: McGraw-Hill/Irwin, 2014.

Business Acumen

Fleisher, C. S., & Bensoussan, B. E., *Business and Competitive Analysis: Effective Application of New and Classic Methods* (2nd ed.). Upper Saddle River, NJ: Pearson, 2015.

Sesil, J. C., *Applying Advanced Analytics to HR Management Decisions: Methods for Selection, Developing Incentives, and Improving Collaboration.* Upper Saddle River, NJ: Pearson, 2014.

Consultation

Kotter, J. P., *Leading Change.* Boston, MA: Harvard Business Review Press, 2012.

Browne, M. N., & Keeley, S. M., *Asking the Right Questions: A Guide to Critical Thinking* (11th ed.). Boston, MA: Pearson, 2014.

Critical Evaluation

Kallet, M., *Think Smarter: Critical Thinking to Improve Problem-Solving and Decision-Making Skills*. Hoboken, NJ: John Wiley & Sons, Inc., 2014.

Levenson, A., *Employee Surveys That Work: Improving Design, Use, and Organizational Impact*. San Francisco, CA: Berrett-Koehler, 2014.

Cultural and Global Effectiveness

Livermore, D., *Leading with Cultural Intelligence: The Real Secret to Success* (2nd ed). New York, NY: AMACOM, 2015.

Sparrow, P., Brewster, C., & Chung, C., *Globalizing Human Resource Management* (2nd ed.). New York, NY: Routledge, 2016.

Communication

Duarte, N., *HBR Guide to Persuasive Presentations*. Boston, MA: Harvard Business Review Press, 2012.

Stone, D., & Heen, S., *Thanks for the Feedback: The Science and Art of Receiving Feedback Well*. New York, NY: Penguin, 2014.

Relationship Management

Fisher, R., Ury, W., & Patton, B., *Getting to Yes: Negotiating Agreement Without Giving In*. New York: Penguin, 2011.

Wheelan, S. A., *Creating Effective Teams: A Guide for Members and Leaders* (5th ed.). Thousand Oaks, CA: SAGE Publications, Inc., 2016.

Talent Acquisition

Heneman III, H. G., Judge, T. A., & Kammeyer-Mueller, J., *Staffing Organizations* (8th ed.). New York, NY: McGraw-Hill, 2015.

Learning & Development

Kirkpatrick, D. L., & Kirkpatrick, J. D., *Evaluating Training Programs: The Four Levels* (3rd ed.). San Francisco, CA: Berrett-Koehler, 2006.

Pollock, R. V. H., Jefferson, A. M., & Calhoun, W. W., *The Six Disciplines of Breakthrough Learning.* (3rd ed.). Hoboken, NJ: John Wiley & Sons, Inc., 2015.

Total Rewards

Martocchio, J. J., *Strategic Compensation: A Human Resource Management Approach* (9th ed.). Hoboken, NJ: Pearson Education, Inc., 2015.

Organizational Effectiveness & Development

Cameron, E., & Green, M., *Making Sense of Change Management: A Complete Guide to the Models, Tools and Techniques of Organizational Change* (4th ed.). London, UK: Kogan Page, 2015.

Levenson, A., *Strategic Analytics: Advancing Strategy Execution and Organizational Effectiveness.* Oakland, CA: Berrett-Koehler Publishers, Inc., 2015.

Workforce Management

Heneman III, H. M., Judge, T. A., & Kammeyer-Mueller, J., *Staffing Organizations* (8th ed.). New York, NY: McGraw-Hill/ Irwin, 2015.

Employee Relations & Labor Relations

Carrell, M. R., & Heavrin, C., *Labor Relations and Collective Bargaining: Private and Public Sectors* (10th ed.). Upper Saddle River, NJ: Prentice Hall, 2012.

HR in the Global Context

Lawler III, E. E., & Boudreau, J. W., *Global Trends in Human Resource Management: A Twenty-Year Analysis.* Stanford, CA: Stanford University Press, 2015.

Sparrow, P., Brewster, C., & Chung, C., *Globalizing Human Resource Management (Global HRM)* (2nd ed.). New York, NY: Routledge, 2016.

Diversity & Inclusion

Bucher, R. D., *Diversity Consciousness: Opening Our Minds to People, Cultures, and Opportunities* (4th ed.). Boston, MA: Pearson, 2015.

Ferdman, B. M., & Deane, B. R. (Eds.), *Diversity at Work: The Practice of Inclusion.* San Francisco, CA: Jossey-Bass, 2014.

Risk Management

Larcker, D. & Tayan, B., *Corporate Governance Matters: A Closer Look at Organizational Choices and Their Consequences* (2nd ed.). Old Tappan, NJ: Pearson FT Press, 2016.

Corporate Social Responsibility

Wheelen, T., Hunger, D., Hoffman, A., & Bamford, C., *Strategic Management and Business Policy: Globalization, Innovation, and Sustainability* (15th ed.). Upper Saddle River, NJ: Pearson, 2014.

U.S. Employment Law & Regulations

Steingold, F., *The Employer's Legal Handbook* (11th ed.). Berkeley, CA: NOLO, 2013

Index

P

PDCs (Professional Development
Credits) 18
Peale, Norman Vincent 55
Pipes, Taylor 38
procrastination 90–94
Professional Development Credits
(PDCs) 18
Prometric 15, 99

S

*SHRM Body of Competency and
Knowledge*™ (SHRM
BoCK™) 3
behavioral competency clusters
of 57
functional areas of 3
key behavioral competencies
of 3, 60
knowledge areas of 60
knowledge domains of 57
studying with 52
SHRM certification
attributes of 8
maintaining 17–18
scholarships 28
SHRM Certification Candidate
Agreement 7
SHRM Certification
Commission 15
SHRM certification exam
administration of 15
answering questions 56, 68
application for 7–8

coverage of 3–10
deadline for 7
eligibility for 5–7
myths about 59
preparation time for 19–20
questions on 11–14
rescheduling 100
scheduling 15
scoring 15–16, 60, 127–128
security 101–103
studying for. *See* studying
*SHRM Certification
Handbook* 100
SHRM Connect online
community 65, 73
SHRM-CP 4. *See also* SHRM
certification exam
accreditation 9
eligibility for 6
SHRM Learning System 26–27
preparation course 40
SHRM-SCP 5. *See also* SHRM
certification exam
accreditation 9
eligibility for 6
situational judgment item (SJI) 12
responses 60
scenarios 58
studying 33
standards
Buros Standards for
Accreditation 9
for Educational and
Psychological Testing 9

Other SHRM Titles

A Manager's Guide to Developing Competencies in HR Staff
Tips and Tools for Improving Proficiency in Your Reports
Phyllis G. Hartman, SHRM-SCP

Actualized Leadership
Meeting Your Shadow and Maximizing Your Potential
William L. Sparks

California Employment Law: A Guide for Employers
Revised and Updated 2018 Edition
James J. McDonald, Jr., JD

Digital HR
A Guide to Technology-Enabled HR
Deborah Waddill, Ed.D.

Extinguish Burnout
A Practical Guide to Prevention and Recovery
Robert Bogue and Terri Bogue

From Hello to Goodbye: Second Edition
Proactive Tips for Maintaining Positive Employee Relations
Christine V. Walters, JD, SHRM-SCP

From We Will to At Will
A Handbook for Veteran Hiring, Transitioning, and Thriving in the Workplace
Justin Constantine with Andrew Morton

Go Beyond the Job Description
A 100-Day Action Plan for Optimizing Talents and Building Engagement
Ashley Prisant Lesko, Ph.D., SHRM-SCP

The HR Career Guide
Great Answers to Tough Career Questions
Martin Yate, CPC

HR on Purpose!!
Developing Deliberate People Passion
Steve Browne, SHRM-SCP

Investing in People
Financial Impact of Human Resource Initiatives, 3rd edition
Wayne F. Cascio, John W. Boudreau, and Alexis A. Fink

Mastering Consultation as an HR Practitioner
Making an Impact on Small Businesses
Jennifer Currence, SHRM-SCP

Motivation-Based Interviewing
A Revolutionary Approach to Hiring the Best
Carol Quinn

The 9 Faces of HR
Discovering HR Disruptors that Add Value, Drive Change, and Champion Innovation
Kris Dunn

The Practical Guide to HR Analytics
Using Data to Inform, Transform, and Empower HR Decisions
Shonna D. Waters, Valerie N. Streets, Lindsay A. McFarlane, and Rachel Johnson-Murray

The Power of Stay Interviews for Engagement and Retention
Second Edition
Richard P. Finnegan

Predicting Business Success
Using Smarter Analytics to Drive Results
Scott Mondore, Hannah Spell, Matt Betts, and Shane Douthitt

The Recruiter's Handbook
A Complete Guide for Sourcing, Selecting, and Engaging the Best Talent
Sharlyn Lauby, SHRM-SCP

The SHRM Essential Guide to Employment Law
A Handbook for HR Professionals, Managers, and Businesses
Charles H. Fleischer, JD

Solve Employee Problems Before They Start
Resolving Conflict in the Real World
Scott Warrick

The Talent Fix
A Leader's Guide to Recruiting Great Talent
Tim Sackett, SHRM-SCP

Books Approved for SHRM Recertification Credits

107 Frequently Asked Questions About Staffing Management, Fiester
(ISBN: 9781586443733)

47 Frequently Asked Questions About the Family and Medical Leave Act, Fiester
(ISBN: 9781586443801)

57 Frequently Asked Questions About Workplace Safety and Security, Fiester
(ISBN: 9781586443610)

97 Frequently Asked Questions About Compensation, Fiester
(ISBN: 9781586443566)

A Manager's Guide to Developing Competencies in HR Staff, Hartman
(ISBN: 9781586444365)

A Necessary Evil: Managing Employee Activity on Facebook, Wright
(ISBN: 9781586443412)

Aligning Human Resources and Business Strategy, Holbeche
(ISBN: 9780750680172)

Applying Critical Evaluation: Making an Impact in Small Business, Currence
(ISBN: 9781586444426)

Becoming the Evidence Based Manager, Latham
(ISBN: 9780891063988)

Being Global: How to Think, Act, and Lead in a Transformed World, Cabrera
(ISBN: 9781422183229)

Black Holes and White Spaces: Reimagining the Future of Work and HR, Boudreau
(ISBN: 9781586444617)

Business Literacy Survival Guide for HR Professionals, Garey
(ISBN: 9781586442057)

Business-Focused HR: 11 Processes to Drive Results, Mondore
(ISBN: 9781586442040)

Calculating Success, Hoffman
(ISBN: 9781422166390)

California Employment Law, Revised and Updated, McDonald
(ISBN: 9781586444815)

Collaborate: The Art of We, Sanker
(ISBN: 9781118114728)

Deep Dive: Proven Method for Building Strategy, Horwath
(ISBN: 9781929774821)

Defining HR Success: 9 Critical Competencies for HR Professionals, Alonso
(ISBN: 9781586443825)

Destination Innovation: HR's Role in Charting the Course, Buhler
(ISBN: 9781586443832)

Developing Business Acumen, Currence
(ISBN: 9781586444143)

Developing Proficiency in HR: 7 Self-Directed Activities for HR Professionals, Cohen
(ISBN: 9781586444167)

Digital HR: A Guide to Technology-Enabled Human Resources, Waddill
(ISBN: 9781586445423)

Diverse Teams at Work: Capitalizing on the Power of Diversity, Gardenswartz
(ISBN: 9781586440367)

Effective Human Resource Management: A Global Analysis, Lawler
(ISBN: 9780804776875)

Emotional Intelligence 2.0, Bradberry
(ISBN: 9780974320625)

Financial Analysis for HR Managers, Director
(ISBN: 9780133925425)

From Hello to Goodbye, 2e, Walters
(ISBN: 9781586444471)

From We Will to at Will: A Handbook for Veteran Hiring, Constantine
(ISBN: 9781586445072)

Give Your Company a Fighting Chance, Danaher
(ISBN: 9781586443658)

Go Beyond the Job Description, Lesko
(ISBN: 9781586445171)

Good People, Bad Managers: How Work Culture Corrupts Good Intentions, Culbert
(ISBN: 9780190652395)

Got a Minute? The 9 Lessons Every HR Professional Must Learn to Be Successful, Dwyer
(ISBN: 9781586441982)

Got a Solution? HR Approaches to 5 Common and Persistent Business Problems, Dwyer
(ISBN: 9781586443665)

Handbook for Strategic HR: Best Practices in Organization Development, Vogelsang
(ISBN: 9780814432495)

Hidden Drivers of Success: Leveraging Employee Insights for Strategic Advantage, Schiemann
(ISBN: 9781586443337)

HR at Your Service: Lessons from Benchmark Service Organizations, Latham
(ISBN: 9781586442477)

HR on Purpose: Developing Deliberate People Passion, Browne
(ISBN: 9781586444259)

HR Transformation: Building Human Resources from the Inside Out, Ulrich
(ISBN: 9780071638708)

HR's Greatest Challenge: Driving the C-Suite to Improve Employee Engagement ..., Finnegan
(ISBN: 9781586443795)

Humanity Works: Merging Technologies and People for the Workforce of the Future, Levit
(ISBN: 9780749483456)

Investing in People: Financial Impact of Human Resource Initiatives, 2e, Boudreau
(ISBN: 9780132394116)

Investing in What Matters: Linking Employees to Business Outcomes, Mondore
(ISBN: 9781586441371)

Leadership from the Mission Control Room to the Boardroom, Hill
(ISBN: 9780998634319)

Leading an HR Transformation, Anderson
(ISBN: 9781586444860)

Leading the Unleadable, Willett
(ISBN: 9780814437605)

Leading with Dignity, Hicks
(ISBN: 9780300229639)

Lean HR: Introducing Process Excellence to Your Practice, Lay
(ISBN: 9781481914208)

Linkage Inc.'s Best Practices for Succession Planning: Case Studies, Research, Models, Tools, Sobol
(ISBN: 9780787985790)

Looking to Hire an HR Leader, Hartman
(ISBN: 9781586443672)

Manager 3.0: A Millennial's Guide to Rewriting the Rules of Management, Karsh
(ISBN: 9780814432891)

Manager Onboarding: 5 Steps for Setting New Leaders Up for Success, Lauby
(ISBN: 9781586444075)

Manager's Guide to Employee Engagement, Carbonara
(ISBN: 9780071799508)

Managing Employee Turnover, Allen
(ISBN: 9781606493403)

Managing the Global Workforce, Caligiuri
(ISBN: 9781405107327)

Managing the Mobile Workforce: Leading, Building, and Sustaining Virtual Teams, Clemons
(ISBN: 9780071742207)

Managing the Older Worker: How to Prepare for the New Organizational Order, Cappelli
(ISBN: 9781422131657)

Mastering Consultation as an HR Practitioner, Currence
(ISBN: 9781586445027)

Measuring ROI in Employee Relations and Compliance, Phillips
(ISBN: 9781586443597)

Motivation-Based Interviewing: A Revolutionary Approach to Hiring the Best, Quinn
(ISBN: 9781586445478)

Multipliers: How the Best Leaders Make Everyone Smarter, Wiseman
(ISBN: 9780061964398)

Negotiation at Work: Maximize Your Team's Skills with 60 High-Impact Activities, Asherman
(ISBN: 9780814431900)

New Power: How Power Works in Our Hyperconnected World, Heimans
(ISBN: 9780385541114)

Nine Minutes on Monday: The Quick and Easy Way to Go from Manager to Leader, Robbins
(ISBN: 9780071801980)

One Life: How Organisations Can Leverage Work-Life Integration, Uhereczky
(ISBN: 9782874035180)

One Strategy: Organizing, Planning and Decision Making, Sinofsky
(ISBN: 9780470560457)

Organizational Design that Sticks, Albrecht
(ISBN: 9781948699006)

Peer Coaching at Work, Parker
(ISBN: 9780804797092)

People Analytics: How Social Sensing Technology Will Transform Business, Waber
(ISBN: 9780133158311)

Perils and Pitfalls of California Employment Law: A Guide for HR Professionals, Effland
(ISBN: 9781586443634)

Point Counterpoint: New Perspectives on People & Strategy, Tavis
(ISBN: 9781586442767)

Point Counterpoint II: New Perspectives on People & Strategy, Vosburgh
(ISBN: 9781586444181)

Practices for Engaging the 21st-Century Workforce, Castellano
(ISBN: 9780133086379)

Predicting Business Success: Using Smarter Analytics to Drive Results, Mondore
(ISBN: 9781586445379)

Preventing Workplace Harassment in a #MeToo World, Dominick
(ISBN: 9781586445539)

Proving the Value of HR: How and Why to Measure ROI, Phillips
(ISBN: 9781586442316)

Reality Based Leadership, Wakeman
(ISBN: 9780470613504)

Reinventing Jobs: A 4-Step Approach for Applying Automation to Work, Jesuthasan
(ISBN: 9781633694071)

Rethinking Retention in Good Times and Bad, Finnegan
(ISBN: 9780891062387)

Social Media Strategies for Professionals and Their Firms, Golden
(ISBN: 9780470633106)

Solving the Compensation Puzzle: Putting Together a Complete Pay and Performance System, Koss
(ISBN: 9781586440923)

StandOut 2.0: Assess Your Strengths, Find Your Edge, Win at Work, Buckingham
(ISBN: 9781633690745)

Stop Bullying at Work, 2e, Daniel
(ISBN: 9781586443856)

Talent, Transformation, and the Triple Bottom Line, Savitz
(ISBN: 9781118140970)

The ACE Advantage: How Smart Companies Unleash Talent for Optimal Performance, Schiemann
(ISBN: 9781586442866)

The Big Book of HR, Mitchell
(ISBN: 9781601631893)

The Circle Blueprint: Decoding the Conscious and Unconscious Factors ..., Skeen
(ISBN: 9781119434856)

The Crowdsourced Performance Review, Mosley
(ISBN: 9780071817981)

The Cultural Fit Factor: Creating an Employment Brand That Attracts ..., Pellet
(ISBN: 9781586441265)

The Definitive Guide to HR Communication, Davis
(ISBN: 9780137061433)

The Employee Engagement Mindset, Clark
(ISBN: 9780071788298)

The EQ Interview: Finding Employees with High Emotional Intelligence, Lynn
(ISBN: 9780814409411)

The Global Challenge: International Human Resource Management, 2nd ed., Evans
(ISBN: 9780073530376)

The Global M&A Tango, Trompenaars
(ISBN: 9780071761154)

The Hard Talk Handbook: The Definitive Guide to Having the Difficult Conversations ..., Metcalfe (ASIN: B07J2C8YF5)

The HR Answer Book, 2e, Smith
(ISBN: 9780814417171)

The HR Career Guide: Great Answers to Tough Career Questions, Yate
(ISBN: 9781586444761)

The HR Insider: How to Land Your Dream Job, and Keep It!, Jeshani
(ISBN: 9781717475565)

The Manager's Guide to HR, 2e, Muller
(ISBN: 9780814433027)

The Performance Appraisal Tool Kit, Falcone
(ISBN: 9780814432631)

The Power of Appreciative Inquiry: A Practical Guide to Positive Change, 2nd ed., Whitney
(ISBN: 9781605093284)

The Power of Stay Interviews for Retention and Engagement, 2e, Finnegan
(ISBN: 9781586445126)

The Practical Guide to HR Analytics, Waters
(ISBN: 9781586445324)

The Recruiter's Handbook, Lauby
(ISBN: 9781586444655)

The SHRM Essential Guide to Employment Law, Fleischer
(ISBN: 9781586444709)

The Square and the Triangle: The Power of Integrating Relationships ..., Stevens
(ISBN: 9781612061474)

The Talent Fix: A Leader's Guide to Recruiting Great Talent, Sackett
(ISBN: 9781586445225)

Thinking in Bets: Making Smarter Decisions When You Don't Have All the Facts, Duke
(ISBN: 9780735216358)

Thrive By Design: The Neuroscience That Drives High-Performance Cultures, Rheem
(ISBN: 9781946633064)

Touching People's Lives: Leaders' Sorrow or Joy, Losey
(ISBN: 9781586444310)

Transformational Diversity, Citkin
(ISBN: 9781586442309)

Transformative HR: How Great Companies Use Evidence-Based Change ..., Boudreau
(ISBN: 9781118036044)

Type R: Transformative Resilience for Thriving in a Turbulent World, Marston
(ISBN: 9781610398060)

Up, Down, and Sideways: High-Impact Verbal Communication for HR Professionals, Buhler
(ISBN: 9781586443375)

View from the Top: Leveraging Human and Organization Capital to Create Value, Wright
(ISBN: 9781586444006)

WE: Men, Women, and the Decisive Formula for Winning at Work, Anderson
(ISBN: 9781119524694)

Weathering Storms: Human Resources in Difficult Times, SHRM
(ISBN: 9781586441340)

What If? Short Stories to Spark Diversity Dialogue, Robbins
(ISBN: 9780891062752)

What Is Global Leadership? 10 Key Behaviors that Define Great Global Leaders, Gundling
(ISBN: 9781904838234)

Winning the War for Talent in Emerging Markets: Why Women are the Solution, Hewlett
(ISBN: 9781422160602)

Work Rules!: Insights from Inside Google That Will Transform How You Live and Lead, Bock
(ISBN: 9781455554799)

CPSIA information can be obtained
at www.ICGtesting.com
Printed in the USA
LVHW080811201121
703957LV00029B/1490